THE NJOMBE ROAD

A Memoir

MARY JO MCMILLIN

With Best Wishes to GHS class of 1959 ~ Mary Jo 2019

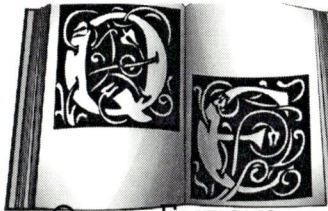

QUITAB EDITIONS

Cover art, interior art, & author photo: © Zach Weiss Photography
    Map, p. 5: ©1960, National Geographic Society
    Original interior photographs by Mary Jo McMillin
Design & layout: Steven Asmussen
Copyediting: Linda E. Kim

Quitab Editions: an imprint of
Glass Lyre Press, LLC
P.O. Box 2693
Glenview, IL 60025

www.GlassLyrePress.com

For David and Catherine

With deep gratitude for my husband, the late James Reiss, who guided this writing project and my first husband, the late Robert Wendel who encouraged our African adventure.

PRAISE FOR *THE NJOMBE ROAD*

Seekers of broader horizons and global understanding, learning as much as they taught, hundreds of Teachers for East Africa answered Kennedy's call to do something for their country. And so, there was Mary Jo McMillin in a remote corner of Tanganyika (soon to be Tanzania), so bedazzled by the unexpected that she felt compelled to retain it by keeping a record of what she experienced, in 2-sided, single-spaced aerogram letters to family 10,000 miles away. Decades later we are now the beneficiaries of that earnest, open and thoughtful account.

—**Henry Hamburger** taught A-level math and physics in Kakamega, Kenya. Following his 36-year academic career, he is treasurer and webmaster for Teachers for East Africa Alumni.

ALSO BY MARY JO MCMILLIN

Mary Jo's Cuisine: A Cookbook
(Orange Frazer Press, 2007)

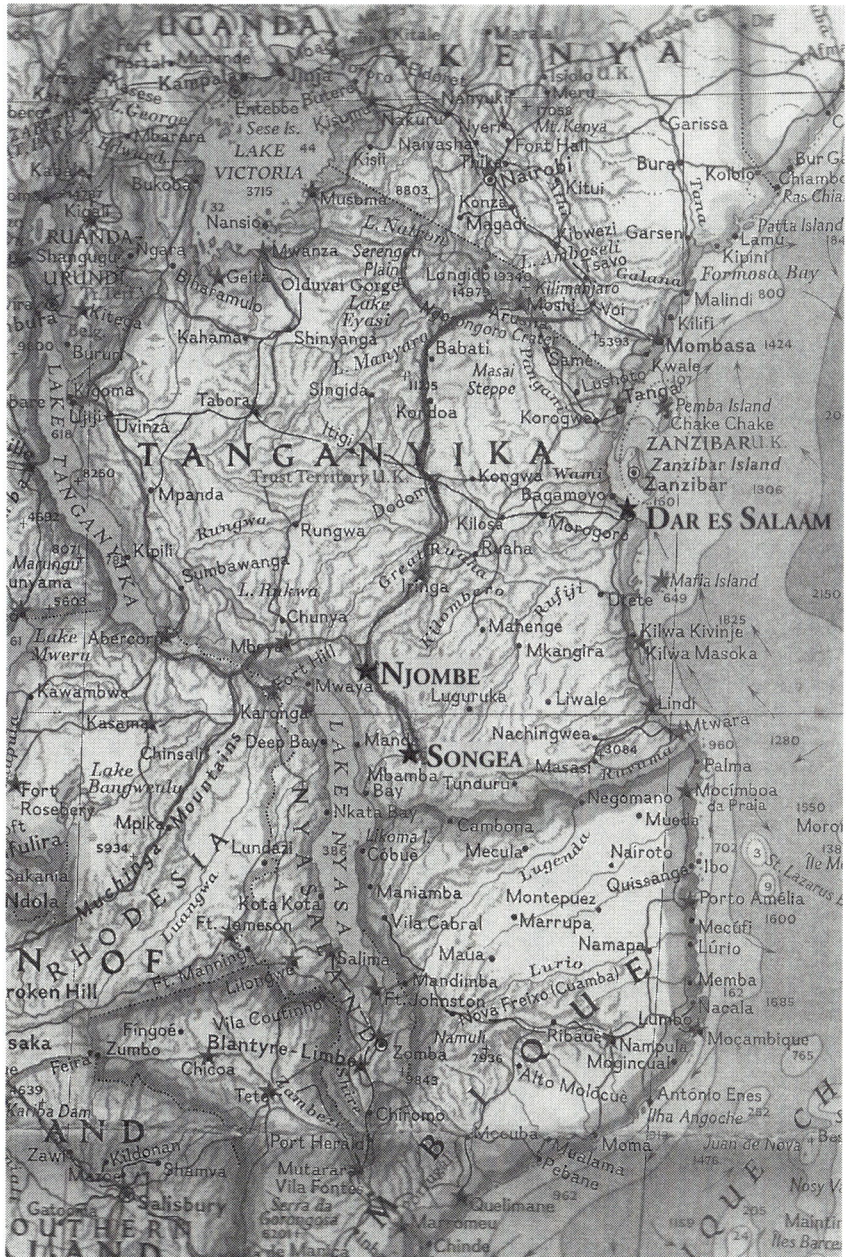

MAP OF TANGANYIKA CA. 1960

CONTENTS

INTRODUCTION

When my mother cleared out the house to move, she mailed me three folders of my old letters. I counted two hundred faded, all but forgotten aerograms filled on both sides, single-spaced, typed on the handbag-sized Olivetti I had carried to East Africa in 1963. As I read through my adventures, I knew I had a story to tell, a slice of history to revive.

At that point I faced the stove full time as chef and owner of a small restaurant, but I kept the idea of a memoir on the back burner. After I sold my business and spent two years writing a cookbook, it was time to go back to the aerograms before their faint print vanished.

Before I wrote these letters home, Bob and I were married in our western Colorado hometown in 1962. He'd been teaching history in southern California for two years, and I still had some college courses to finish for my B.A.. We spent our first year together in Torrance, California where I took classes at Long Beach State while he continued at the local high school. We dreamed of traveling abroad and, like thousands, were spellbound by JFK's challenge to "ask not what your country can do for you—ask what you can do for your country." Fired up with missionary zeal and wanderlust, we applied to teach in a program sponsored by the Agency for International Development.

In May 1963 a telegram arrived announcing our acceptance into Teachers for East Africa. Columbia University Teachers College, in conjunction with the U.S. government and East African countries, trained and placed teachers in Ugandan, Kenyan and Tanganyikan secondary schools. We would spend six weeks at Columbia in New York City studying customs, language and history in preparation for our assignment.

At twenty-two, I envisioned the continent of Africa mysteriously locked between the majesty of Tutankhamen's Egypt and the darkness of Vachel Lindsay's then-popular poem, "The Congo." The emerging nations of Uganda, Tanganyika and Kenya were names that sent me to the encyclopedia. I didn't know Nairobi from Timbuktu. Suddenly I was on an adventure halfway around the world; I would be an outsider and for the first time a minority. I would be away for a long time, with no instant communication and sporadic mail. I was aware of the Serengeti, Hemingway's wild-game hunts and the legendary "Dr. Livingston, I presume." Nonetheless, I had no concept of what it would be to live in the hinterland five hundred miles southwest of Dar es Salaam.

Wedged between Kenya and Mozambique, Tanganyika—now The United Republic of Tanzania—is perhaps the least known of the former British East African countries. Tanzania is one of the most poverty-stricken countries in Africa. At twice the size of California, in 1963 Tanganyika had just over ten million inhabitants. The world's second largest body of fresh water, Lake Victoria, straddles Tanzania's northwest border. Northern highlands claim Africa's highest peak, Mount Kilimanjaro, and lower mountains in the south fringe Mozambique. Scrubby hills, arid plains and grassy savannas fill the expansive center, while tropical vegetation clings to the coast. Subsistence agriculture has controlled the economy for generations, with scattered larger scale farming of sisal, pyrethrum, copra and coffee.

Tanganyika's political leader in the Sixties, Julius Nyerere, was a progressive intellectual who feared he failed. He rallied his young nation in the spirit of family-hood. He believed hard-working families led to strong communities and strong communities would make up a united, independent country. As years passed, fuel crises, drought, famine, and international struggles left Nyerere's dream in the dust.

Between 1963 and '65, however, Tanganyika's cooperative movement flourished, with divisiveness needling its core. The infrastructure of this former German colony and then British territory relied on European-style administration, yet the struggling young nation couldn't help looking to rising communist powers untainted with colonialism. As the government teetered between East and West, most people in the bush lived an almost primeval life.

This book is no Isak Dinesen *Out of Africa* romance. The highs and lows of life in a foreign country, no matter how fascinating, turn into humdrum routines. We experienced a muddled political scene, not unlike what we see in Africa nowadays. In the early Sixties before the civil rights movement in America, the word *Negro* was commonly used. It was not a term of derision; it was simply before "Black" or "African-American" came into vogue. Likewise, *Moslem* was the common usage descriptor for a follower of Islam in the decades before Islamic groups favored "Muslim." Bob and I were posted at a government boarding school for boys, and the use of the word *boy* refers to our students, our household helper and neighboring children, purely and simply as young males, never in a condescending manner. Similarly, we toured South Africa during apartheid. We weren't there to stand in judgment; we traveled as naïve observers. I let the people talk and listened to what they said.

The foods I encountered, as well as the basic meals I needed to produce, challenged my passion for cooking. Ventures into the culinary life of the Indian diaspora saved me from boredom and loneliness. Cooking in Africa kept me busy and set me on the path that became my vocation.

Now, after more than five decades from the day I set foot in Africa, I wonder about former students. I remember Michael, Massudi and Zuberi. Did they become national leaders? I wonder if Joseph and Lucus are still alive. I think of our headmaster, Paul, and hope he has had a good life. I see on the Internet that the Peramiho Mission thrives. Does our yellow house still stand on the Songea Secondary School compound?

When I came to the end of my letters, I realized there was information I did not have. There were missing pages, gaps I couldn't fill from memory. Who was chosen Miss Songea at Saba Saba? Where did Pillay go? Who became the next postmaster? What about parts of our village we never saw? What about the future plans for Mlale?—and the list goes on. Like life itself, there's always more than one person's vision takes in. This book presents a view from a single window. I use the present tense to create an illusion that lets the reader observe the action as it unfolds. I've strung together passages from my letters and omitted family chatter. Perhaps my journalistic chronicle of events, scrupulous in its observation of the panorama around me is a genre that hasn't been exploited recently as much as the introspective memoir. Over the centuries, however, chronicles have served generations of readers eager to ferret out the facts of history.

As diehard teammates Bob and I completed our African adventure. We returned to the U.S. in the summer of 1965 and both went on for graduate degrees at our alma mater, the University of Northern Colorado. We had two children, a son and a daughter. After twenty-four years, we separated. Bob was chair of his university's Department of Teacher Education. I stepped into cook's clogs.

When I was a graduate assistant in Greeley, Colorado, one afternoon as I sat at a study table in the Carter Hall Library my English professor, George Gates, stopped to chat. He recalled the occasional letters I'd mailed him from Africa. He narrowed his gaze, peering through pale pink plastic framed glasses and grasped the bowl of his corncob pipe. He challenged me, "You must write, Mary Jo."

I hesitated, like Jonah. "What shall I write?"

In his Missouri drawl he replied, "You will write about *Ton•gahn• yee•ka.*"

JULY 1963

Out the window across the street there's a sidewalk edged by a shoulder-high chain-link fence. On the other side of the fence a rocky cliff overlooks Harlem, where many-storied buildings bunch like stacked boxes. Lines of multicolored laundry top steaming, tar-papered roofs. Smokestacks, skyscrapers, a cathedral tower etch the skyline fading into industrial shadows. At night apartment lights shimmer and neon blinks while above everything a full moon crests the dark.

We stroll the neighborhood, shopping, cooling off. The stores are small, cluttered. Basement delivery entrances rise cellar-like at the sidewalks' edges, and sliding iron gates shutter locked doors. Matchbox food markets, drug stores and snack bars line every block. Prices are steep: with luck chicken is forty-nine cents a pound, lettuce thirty-nine cents a head. When we walk past apartment steps, old folks the color of smoky brick perch silent, staring. Children play on the sidewalk or in the street while mothers sit at windows, leaning out.

Tuesday it rains. I run outside and stand in the downpour. Later I wash my hair and take a warm shower, but the next morning I wake with a sore throat. By Thursday night I'm in bed on the verge of death. The monster fills my throat, moves into my head and advances toward my chest. A nurse gives me nose drops and ghastly cough syrup at the college clinic.

Sick as I am, three of us go to the theater: my first Broadway play, *Who's Afraid of Virginia Woolf?* In the mob at Times Square we ogle Cleopatra's flashing breasts and the smoke-puffing camel.

Friday evening a friend from the city invites us to dinner. As I step into her spacious duplex on Lexington Avenue, I want to ask if we can stay the night. We leave at midnight; outside her building a crowd gathers around somebody lying on the pavement with blood running down his neck. I clutch Bob's arm as we hurry to the bus stop.

To reach the Upper West Side, we need a transfer. We board the wrong bus, which, instead of taking us up the hill to Morningside Heights, drives into the heart of Harlem. Gangs of T-shirted men loiter by parked cars, couples brawl on apartment steps, saxophone wails filter from bars, while children play hopscotch on the sidewalk. Not only am I blond and white, I'm wearing a white skirt, white shoes and a light blue blouse. The bus driver seems oblivious to our anxiety but tells us the nearest place to get off. We're only a few blocks from home, but those blocks traverse Morningside Park. As we step off the bus, a shriveled prune of a woman takes my arm, looks me in the eye and whispers, "Don't go through that park; they'll kill you in there!" I shudder as we beeline to the nearest cab stand and find a taxi.

***

Tall, lanky, with a Marine colonel bearing, having grown up on a Sacramento Valley walnut ranch, our housemate Bill looks at home in safari khaki. In gypsy skirts and headbands Kat spends hours on the couch, nursing baby Chris. Kat fills the sink with dirty dishes, leaves toys, puddles, and burp clothes on the living room floor. She vacuums once in a while, while I scrub the kitchen and clean the dining room every evening. We're splitting the grocery bills, but I feel peeved when Bill wolfs down two chicken breasts and a thigh while I have two wings.

With one week of orientation left, we keep hearing the same stuff about "cultural guidelines" and "the need to learn Swahili." Only Margaret Mead gives two memorable lectures. We sit breathlessly as she marches to the lectern at the front of the hall in a plain black shirt-dress and black granny shoes, a sturdy black walking stick stomping at her side.

AUGUST 1963

We're pleased to learn we've been placed in the Tanganyika group, and we're hoping to be posted in the northern highlands. Tanganyika's educational system follows British standards under the new independent government led by Julius Nyerere.

There will be no jet mainliner for our group of fifty-nine in the 1963 wave of Teachers For East Africa, a USAID-sponsored project bound for twenty to twenty-four month stints at state-run East African schools. We're hired as temporary civil servants to the local government. We're expected to live on the economy while a U.S. stipend awaits us as a bonus on our completion of a tour of duty.

We're chartered on an old four-engine prop, a Capitol Airways Constellation. We'll have forty hours en route and four touchdowns for fuel. With fourteen children in tow, six are under two. The plane is not air-conditioned; there will be minimal food and a limited supply of water. Our flight schedule:

Depart Idlewild 3:00 p.m. Sunday August 11th

*(Although not listed on the printed itinerary,
we remember stopping first in Gander)*

Arrive Shannon 7 a.m. August 12th

Depart Shannon 8:30 a.m.

Arrive Cairo 10:30 p.m. August 12th

Depart Cairo midnight

Arrive Entebbe 8 a.m. August 13th

Leave Entebbe 9:30 a.m.

Arrive Nairobi 11:00 a.m.

Leave Nairobi 12:30 p.m.

Arrive Dar es Salaam 2:30 p.m.

***

We've landed in the city of pharaohs, home of the pyramids. It's too dark to see anything. When I walk down the steps of the plane, my skirt balloons with furnace-like heat. Inside the airport I see a toilet with two places for feet in front of a hole in the floor. There's only one room in the terminal unlocked at this time of night. Turbaned stewards hurry through the crowd while African children cling to their veiled mothers burdened with armloads of packages and paper bags.

Drugged with Dramamine, I doze through the Entebbe and Nairobi stops. I'm still light-headed when we reach Dar es Salaam, named by early Arab traders as "haven of peace." Our hotel veranda looks out on a cove-like harbor where yachts, sailboats and dhows skim the water and a cargo ship stands at anchor.

We're lodged in European luxury near the beach at the New Africa Hotel. Caned split reed rockers line the front porch, and inside a thin runner of red, black and ivory Persian carpet softens the wide wooden hall floor. No screened windows lighten our room, but large air spaces open in the wall eight feet above the floor. We spend our first night under mosquito netting suspended from the ceiling and draped around each bed. I hear no sirens or cars. I'm lulled by crickets' cheeping and waves lapping at the shore. About five a.m. cat-like animals let out long, high-pitched squeals; near six light breaks and the hotel workers arrive. We hear a singsong of chatter we can't understand. At six-thirty, a serving boy raps at our door announcing, *Hodi?* (May I come in?) We answer, *Karibu*, and he offers a tray with steaming cups of tea. We shake out our shoes to make sure no scorpions have crawled in.

The dining room offers cornflakes, scrambled eggs and toast with marmalade for breakfast. Lunch features a spicy curry with sweet fruit chutney, and dinner turns into five courses of drab British-type hotel food. The sliced white bread is soft and plain, but the butter is sweetly delicious. Tonight we have a bland broth and noodle soup, roast beef with boiled carrots and potatoes, an orange pudding dessert and cheese with crackers. Everything is cooked to death, and there are no salads. We find the small, green bananas much sweeter than those in the States. Oranges are yellow and lemons are light green.

Throughout the hotel stewards squat in the halls, scrubbing floors with hand-cloths or sweeping with six-inch-handled brooms. From early morning tea till after dinner, a young man swings an electric polisher back and forth as its motor drones. I ask our room steward if he'll clean the floor. I assume he'll swish it up with a dust mop, but no, he removes the furniture, rugs, suitcases and sets about the scrub and wax routine. I feel dreadful about the mess I've caused and don't know how long it will take. By evening, both the floor and all our shoes are shining with the strong smell of polish. My first purchase today is a Swahili dictionary.

While Bob is in session at the ministry, I set out to explore Independence Avenue. I feel taken back into a pioneer settlement by corner food shops that display little boxes of Kellogg's corn flakes and Coca-Cola bottles in the window. Inside, tea packets are stacked, along with jars of preserved ginger; a locked glass box holds bubble gum and Gillette Blue Blades.

An African woman dressed in a long green gown and black veil wears pink plastic sandals and carries a blue plastic purse loaded with a large thermos bottle. Along the walkways barefoot boys squat by charcoal braziers roasting maize or sweet potatoes to sell alongside stacks of peanuts or mounds of popcorn. Beggars reach out, and I don't know what to do. I'm astonished at the British chaps striding about in short shorts. A heavy outhouse odor combined with chili and garlic fills the congested streets. The smell comes and goes; after a while I don't notice it.

Ministry of Education officials greet us this evening. Mr. Sutton gently informs Bob and me that we've been assigned to Songea (pronounced "Song-GAY-uh"), the southernmost school in the bush, Post Fourteen. Oh my God, this is the spot everyone scoffed at during training—the most remote school, the place that once took fourteen days to reach. Our colleagues avoid our eyes and offer us pity.

We have a new home address: c/o Songea Secondary School, P.O. Box 2, Songea, Tanganyika, East Africa! The headmaster is P.O. Box 1; the teachers are P.O. Box 2. We're beginning to hear a few good things about Songea's neck of the bush. Its southern highlands elevation is five thousand feet; it has cool nights, pleasant days and good soil for gardening. There's supposed to be a plentiful food supply, nearby medical facilities, and the teachers' houses have fireplaces. A sixty-five-year-old German Benedictine mission compound is sixteen miles from the school. Songea is the headquarters for the Ruvuma region bordering Lake Nyasa and Mozambique in the southwest corner of the country. Songea town has no electricity or telephones.

All cars here are right-hand drive; traffic runs English-style, on the left side of the road. We've settled on a VW. Land Rovers and Volkswagens are the only sensible cars for our area, and the Land Rover is beyond our means. There isn't much selection and the prices seem high, but we purchase a used '63 bug with three thousand "city miles"; we name her Zelda. The insurance is government controlled, and it, too, seems exorbitant, but we're now tagged with a license plate:

EAT

T D 6323

The "EAT" stands for East Africa Tanganyika.

We leave Dar for Songea Sunday morning and hope to reach the halfway point, Iringa, three hundred and fifteen miles inland. The road is good with tarmac nearly half the way and a washboard dirt track the rest of the distance. We've been told to watch for big game on the Morogoro-Iringa section, so I glue my eyes to the bush for hours, but all I see is one gray monkey. I notice maize, banana, sugar cane, castor beans, papaya and mangos growing in native plots. We pass plantation-size stretches of wattle and sisal. Giant baobab trees break up vast stretches of savanna. This indigenous tree with its massive trunk, which may be large enough for twenty people to circle, lives for thousands of years. It is sometimes called the upside-down tree, since it appears to have been pulled up and planted with its roots on top. Its trunk may be thirty feet in diameter, but its scraggly, often leafless top tufts out modestly.

Iringa looks like a village high in the South American Andes. The roads are treacherous; it's biting cold, and the native people walk around wrapped in blankets. We spend the night at the White Horse Inn run by two Greek men. Our $1.14 evening dinner includes leek soup, bread and butter, mixed grill, cheese, crackers and coffee.

The next morning on the way to Songea, Bob hugs the wheel. I grasp the handle above the car pocket, bracing back in the seat to steady the luggage, as we ride the wild mustang another two hundred and fifty–plus miles. The road, pocked with ruts and sand traps, is barely wide enough for one car. We feel lost on a hunting trail, only to pass a few white painted milestones or occasionally a washed out wooden sign with the words, Songea Road. We meet two cars, two buses and a truck between Songea and Njombe, our midway point.

The landscape unfolds in a kaleidoscope of green; the soil is orange, umber or smoky gray. Again we see no animals, though a few people walk on the road. PWD (Public Works Department) has a couple repair crews out, but we seldom see them working. Three huts appear in a clearing where a lone woman and child, both wrapped in dusty black cloth, stand by a dark clay pot over a fire. Across the road four men sit drinking together on large logs under a low thatched roof with no walls. We climb the Lukumburu escarpment, and late in the afternoon arrive at what will become our hometown.

The Songea Secondary School compound spreads over a hillside three and a half miles from the town. The soil is red and most of the trees resemble scrub oaks. Everything is dusty here, though it's cool enough to wear sweaters most of the day. We've left tropical vegetation behind, but still see banana plants, mango and papaya trees.

Rich and Vic, two American TEAers, offer us a room until our house is ready. We don't know how long it will take the slow-moving PWD crew to finish our new stuccoed, cinderblock house, but it will have plenty of space. We'll have an apartment-size bottled gas stove, running water, inside plumbing and electricity for lights from 6:30 to 11:30 in the evening when the school generator operates. The house has a counterless kitchen with pantry, three bedrooms, one bathroom and a sitting room/dining room. There's a fireplace in the sitting room,. The rent for our basic house with locally built wooden furniture will be $26 a month.

*　*　*

Our first night here the African headmaster, Paul Mhaike, invites us for dinner. His red clay brick residence, a mile from the school toward the village, is grander than most houses in the vicinity. Paul has no electricity, but warm kerosene lamps light his living room/ dining room. Inside, pastel colors cover mud-plastered walls, and the underside of a corrugated iron roof forms a low ceiling. Yellow muslin pillows cushion plain wooden chairs, and hand-embroidered placemats decorate the table. Paul's wife, the first chubby African woman I've seen, speaks no English. We practice a few words of Swahili and flash lots of smiles.

Mrs. Mhaike doesn't eat with us but passes dishes to a serving boy through an opening in the wall between the kitchen and dining room. I'm disappointed she's gone to such lengths to prepare a European meal when I'm eager to taste local dishes. She serves soup made from a packaged mix, stewed beef with rice, cooked cabbage, beer, tinned fruit cocktail and lemonade.

Paul tells us he'll be leaving soon on a fellowship at Pittsburgh's Duquesne University. We'll have an acting headmaster.

***

Our state-run boys' school has two hundred and eighty students and eleven teachers; five teachers are American, one is English, two are Asian, three are African. This morning we tour the campus of red mud-brick school buildings and join the staff for tea, a strong black brew mixed with undiluted sweetened condensed milk. A small library has a copy of *The Encyclopedia Britannica.* The laboratory under construction is poorly designed; its wall between the window side and the class space makes it dark inside. Plus, there's no electricity for lights during the day. Bob will teach world history, African history, and English. He's expected to take care of the library and is house-master for the Zulu House dormitory. He will be on a rota for dining hall inspection and bed check, which one faculty member performs every day. We're advised to hire a houseboy to help with washing and cleaning and to add a scrap of cash to the local economy. So we decide to employ Saidi, who works part time for Rich and Vic, once we move into our own house. He will work for R and V in the morning and come to us in the afternoon.

The schoolboys' dormitories, communal bunkhouses, are long bare rooms with beds jutting from the walls. Each boy has a hook above his cot for clothing and a bed-width wooden shelf for books, a metal dinner plate, soup bowl and teacup. Unpolished, hand-hewn wooden tables and benches fill the dining hall. When I ask about the cooks, Rich tells me they were found stealing food, so the school gardeners have been put in the kitchen and the cooks in the garden.

The boys get maize flour gruel for breakfast; lunch and dinner mean soup made from dry beans slowly cooked in water with a smidgeon of fat and curry powder. Twice a week a rationed amount of meat goes into the bean stew. The soup/stew is served with rice or *ugali*, a porridge made from ground corn or cassava. The only milk the boys get is the sweetened condensed goo mixed into their morning tea. In their spic and span school uniforms striding up the path to class, the boys give no inkling of how dirt-simply they live.

Jacaranda trees with feathery leaves and lacy purple blossoms line the parade ground in front of the school office where the boys march with the pipe and drum band for inspection every Saturday morning. Huge green-leaved poinsettia bushes reach as high as the windows flanking the north side of the science laboratory. Older school buildings are whitewashed mud brick, and the newer faculty houses are stuccoed cinderblock. There's no lawn on the dry playing field, but neat rows in the school garden offer fresh vegetables. Packed dirt lanes connect the low, one-story classroom buildings and the teachers' ranch-style bungalows surrounding the cantonment-like school compound.

* * *

We drive into Songea town, with its branch of the Standard Bank, two dingy three-pump petrol stations, a post office, a prison, a market square and three dusty *dukas* (shops), plus a scattering of closet-like shops. I want to look for fabric for chair cushions. Each merchant has the same selection: black, white, or a bright orange, chartreuse and violet print.

The three *dukas* around the mud-packed market square supply such basic household necessities as tin buckets, flashlights, nails, and cloth. This is not a place to find a floor mop, a lampshade or packaged spices, but I discover Betty Crocker boxed piecrust mix and Ritz Crackers that must be five years old, along with a few tins of fruit, sausages and tomato paste.

The *dukas* are unlit one-room general stores whose owners usually live in back. On one side out-of-reach shelves hold bolts of cloth. Hardware, tools, rope and saucepans hang from the ceiling. Scratched, locked, glass-topped counters contain sundries such as toothpaste and dime store cosmetics. Candy, raisins and whole spices fill glass jars. In corners burlap bags bulge with onions, flour, rice, beans and coconuts. Nothing has a marked price, so we save receipts to avoid being overcharged. Pardhan's is the best-stocked Asian shop, with two glass cases for toiletries, sewing supplies and candies. Heradia's shop is smaller, darker, but cheaper. The native-run Co-op, is smaller still, wooden-counter-basic, and has the best prices for sugar, salt, rice, tea and Danish dry milk. With no refrigeration in the *dukas*, all fresh produce or meat comes from the morning market or traveling vendors.

I borrow a shopping basket from Rich until I buy my own loosely woven reed floppy basket with twisted sisal handles in the market square. The shopkeeper scoops dry goods like rice, salt or sugar from barrels, bins or bags with metal hand shovels and weighs amounts in the pan of a balance scale with iron bars set on the opposing side. Once my rice is weighed, he twirls a sheet of newspaper into a cone, twists the bottom point, pours in the rice and tucks in the top flaps. Lined up on the counter my newsprint triangles of salt, sugar and rice go into my basket only after I hand over the proper amount of cash and accept his hand-written chit or bill of sale.

***

In cities, small towns and tiny hamlets, Indians keep the shops. Once displaced persons after the British government brought workers from India into East Africa by the boatload to build the railways, many remained. They built a middle class niche as traders and merchants. They're quick and clever with money and thrive in their secure family compounds. Occasionally I see Indian women in the market, but I get the impression that they are totally consumed with the major tasks of cooking and maintaining the households for large extended families.

Africans occupy the top and bottom rungs of the social ladder. They're the government leaders, regional commissioners, school directors as well as the masses of poor farmers and trades-people, while shop-keepers in every village and outpost are Indians.

*　*　*

We don't know the population of Songea since many small villages cluster nearby. A village means anything from a family group of three or four huts to a town with a post office. This area is densely populated, and the large Benedictine mission not far away has ten thousand communicants within a ten-mile radius. Subsistence farming is the way of life here. On their little *shambas* (garden plots), locals grow cassava—a starchy yam-like root, maize, vegetables and fruit. Many households own a few goats, tokens of family wealth and dowries.

So few cars rattle through the village that we often honk our way through throngs of pedestrians, cyclists, cows and chickens when we drive into town. There's no need to use turning signals, since there's no one to signal to, and it usually doesn't matter which side of the road we drive on as long as we hit the left whenever we see an approaching dust cloud.

September 1963

We wake later than usual on this first Sunday in our new home. In the afternoon we walk up one of the paths beyond the school. Africans out for Sunday strolls greet us; even young girls giggle *Jambo* (Hello) as they scurry around us. We pass mud huts where goats rest, chickens scratch, and a few older men or women sit gnawing sticks of sugar cane. From neighboring hills we hear drumming and singing, which announce a wedding celebration.

After a late Sunday lunch in our windowless dining room—glass panes are weeks away in shipment from Dar, so for now we're boarded up—we enjoy tea and coconut cream pie in front of a crackling fire. We beat the bugs to the light and find that elevating the wood on large rocks allows enough air circulation for a tidy blaze.

***

We take the winding dirt road west of the village to Peramiho, the German Benedictine Mission. Our car is not empty. Whenever travel word gets out, someone needs a ride. Today's passenger is Saidi's "mother"—meaning anyone from Saidi's aunt to his great-grandmother. She hopes to see a doctor at the mission hospital, and she presents us with the gift of an egg. After sixteen dust-filled miles, we spy the redbrick cathedral's steeple and the cattle barns' iron rooftops. From the parched bush all at once we enter a manicured, fairy tale–like Swiss village.

We leave Saidi's "mother" at the hospital. Its red tile floor is scrubbed and polished to a T. We meet doctors and nuns in spotless white, only to gasp when we're shown the room with a wall-mounted X-ray machine able to take a picture of the whole body at once.

Everywhere people are on task. Inside the Bishop-director's carpeted office we sit alongside a telegraph machine and an electric typewriter. The director in a long black cassock, wearing wire-rimmed glasses, has the look of German propriety, clean-shaven with brushed brown hair. He offers us thimbles of wine as he describes the mission's training programs. We look in on the tailoring shop with its rows of electric Pfaff sewing machines and two boys pressing clothes with electric irons.

Our guide says Bob can purchase a pair of wash-type trousers for about $1.14 or a pair of fancier slacks for $1.50, only they would come with buttons instead of a zipper. In the cobbler's shop boys operate Singer shoe-sewing machines and whirling buffers. The Africans who show us about are peacock-proud of their work. We pause inside the vast cathedral that serves thousands. The Peramiho compound generates enough electricity for street lamps at night!

* * *

Rather than send Saidi out with a basket and money for carrots Thursday afternoon, I decide to go along. We cross our backyard, the school soccer field and enter a small community. Near the goats and chickens, earthen cooking pots line the side of a house. We can't find a gardener. We pass a man building wooden benches in an open-sided shelter. We meet the "mother" of the houseboy who works for another teacher. The houses have thatched roofs, swatches of red or yellow paint, and mismatched curtains swinging in glassless windows.

Saidi takes me to the house of a *fundi* (a craftsperson, this man is a tailor) who sits in the corner of his dim workroom treadling his old Singer. In tattered yellow trousers, a dirty pink shirt, and a bright

26

blue sweater vest, he wears a white embroidered skullcap. Here men usually have on hats; we seldom see them without caps or fezzes. When our *fundi* understands we'd like to buy vegetables, he puts aside his sewing, picks up a large knife, and we set out for the garden.

Across an arid field, down a prickly hillside, we troop to a clearing near the river, really a smallish stream. Garden plots abound, each belonging to a different person. Some have plants just coming up, and others show a bounty of harvest-ready vegetables. Only cabbage and onions grow in the *fundi's* plot. I return home with a large cabbage and four good-sized onions in my basket for about 17 cents.

Bob used to think cabbage was solely for coleslaw, but now we have it cooked, casseroled and souped. There are decent tomatoes in Songea's market, and I've been using lettuce freely when it comes from nearby gardens. When I wash the lettuce I add a couple teaspoons of chlorine bleach or a small sprinkling of Tide—found in local shop—to the water.

The market beef comes without a scrap of fat. Chunks of meat are hacked from the freshly killed carcass of a Zebu cow each morning. All cuts outside of the fillet are called "steak" no matter whether it's shin, shoulder or flank. The liver and the fillet are the choice pieces, snatched up soon after the market opens. All cuts of meat go for the same price per pound, and sheets of newspaper make up any packaging. Thanks to our meat grinder and pressure cooker, we've had delicious meals from this tough local beef. I hear every now and then goat is available in the market, though it's called mutton, and we wonder if it will taste like lamb.

In the shops near the market, I stock up on a five-pound tin of powdered whole milk from Denmark, canned dry yeast from Holland and good Kenyan flour. Of course our most basic item, water, must be boiled. All water for drinking is simmered for ten minutes before it is poured into a filtering device, a two-part aluminum barrel that looks like a party-sized coffee percolator. The bottom section is the water reservoir and the top section holds an upright two-inch-in-diameter porous ceramic column. The water passes through the ceramic filter to remove further impurities. The contraption sits on top of our wire mesh covered "food safe" and must be filled every day and scrubbed out occasionally.

* * *

Bob's picking up broadcasts on his transistor radio. We hear English language programs from Dar's Radio Tanganyika, Radio Peking, Voice of America, Radio South Africa, as well as French bits from the Congo.

* * *

It's early spring here. By midday the sky is clear blue with puffy clouds, or wispy streaks. Even if the afternoon darkens, we know it will not rain for weeks.

Our evening watch lasts from six to six-thirty when the horizon ribbons with delicate pinks, purples and reds. The sun, glowing like a burning lump of coal, expands and brightens as it sinks. It rests on the western sky's rim for a glittering moment. Then all at once it drops below the horizon, and mauve streaks fade into blue-gray.

As twilight falls, we survey the sky, free of telephone poles and wires. The darkness settles in pure black, the stars polished diamonds, the Milky Way wide and white. The past few nights a giant grapefruit of a moon never shrinks as it glides across the star-swept arch of night. Under the full moon, we don't need a flashlight when we walk out in the evening.

* * *

Early in the term our schoolboys group into tribes to prepare traditional dances. After days of practice they dance on Saturday afternoon. The soccer field becomes a performing arena where villagers, teachers and a motley assortment of friends line up on the dry grass strip to watch. Some boys have put together costumes; others stay with school uniforms. Most use the same instruments: drums, sticks, police-whistles and pipes. Each of the twelve tribes is allowed fifteen minutes, but nearly every group has to be pushed from the field when their time is up. They're accustomed to dancing for hours on end. Their drums throb, and their whistles squeal. They clamp the whistles between their teeth and blow in sharp bursts while they shuffle and shake. One group wears small vests and matching bloomers, while a dancer on stilts is the star performer twirling, bouncing and shimmying as he perches on wooden duck legs about four feet off the ground. The government fears many of these native dances are dying out, but this is not true after what we've seen today.

* * *

Sunday's walk takes us by coffee *shambas* terraced on the hillside. We notice people working the fields, yet everything is so quiet we can almost hear the clouds pass. In these hills small mud and thatch cabins blend into the bush, and we hardly see villages till we step into them.

* * *

As the locals repeat what sounds like a motto, *bado kidogo* (in a little while), we still have no windows in our sitting room. I've gathered flowers and made yellow doilies to liven up the place before inviting the bachelor teachers for afternoon tea. Our guests consume the orange cake and the Swedish coffee ring I've baked as though they haven't had sweets in years.

* * *

In mid-September our sea freight arrives. Seems like we brought enough towels for a regiment but very few sheets, only one tablecloth and no hot pads. We're as excited as kids at Christmas as we dive into the box and tuck things away in drawers.

***

Mid-term break begins Wednesday morning when we set off in Zelda for Mbamba Bay and Lake Nyasa. We travel with three grinning schoolboys who haven't been home since June. The road is rough but dry and we cover the one hundred and ten miles in five hours; the bus making the same trip that day takes fifteen hours. We drive above a timberline that reminds us of Colorado's Loveland Pass. Volcanic boulders clutter moonscape-like sandy soil. On lower slopes tree towers form a lacy canopy that sifts sunlight into shadowy patterns on the underlying grass. As we pass forested areas, we glimpse pine and eucalyptus marked for timber cutting. Clusters of huts and small villages with *shambas* perch on hillsides or dot ravines. Coffee shrubs flourish in the mountains. Close to the lake the primary crop is cassava, a starchy tuber, ground into meal and cooked with water to form the local staple porridge, *ugali*.

As we putter up one last rocky escarpment, the boys shout when they see the expanse of Lake Nyasa, its ocean-like brilliance framed by lava cliffs. We try to drive one schoolboy an extra twenty miles, but the narrow rocky road is too much for VW Zelda. He'll probably have to walk those twenty miles, yet no doubt he's done it many times, and he'll see friends along the way.

Mbamba Bay is little more than half-a-dozen square mud brick cottages, a post office and two one-room shops near the lazy African lull of a white sand beach. What a perfect spot for a swim, I think, until a chilly gust sweeps in. Most fishermen must be out on the lake or napping; I'm hoping to see fresh fish but only find a couple of canoes rocking by the shore while three men sit on the beach mending nets. With no lodgings in the village, we've made arrangements to spend the night at the Roman Catholic mission of Nangombo four miles away.

* * *

We find the mission in time for afternoon tea. When a bell rings we follow two priests in overalls into a dining room for a welcome spread of bread, butter, jam, sausage, fruit and tea. Nangombo is smaller than Peramiho and more remote. It houses both a primary school and a domestic—home economics—school for older girls, as well as a hospital, carpentry shop, cows, chickens and a walled garden.

I'm surprised when Bob and I are ushered into separate bedrooms. I struggle to blow out the kerosene lamp; I burn my hand and melt a pair of nylon socks. As I climb under my mosquito net, flashlight in hand, I meet a cockroach that sends me flying into Bob's room—though I can't stay with him in a cot. I don't sleep that night but curl into a ball and wait for the clock to chime every hour.

* * *

We prepare to return to Songea in the morning and meet our schoolboy, Yohanna, who brings us a chicken. He means the young hen as a gift for dinner, but we think we'll keep her on a string by the storehouse and hope for fresh eggs. Only Yohanna accompanies us back home, so we have a chatterbox of information all the way. After a few miles I beg Bob to stop and turn back toward a statuesque woman balancing a load of maize meal on her head. She's wearing an ivory bracelet on her upper arm. All at once I covet her bracelet, although I could never wear it against my pale skin. The piece is magnificent, stained with a yellowed patina, and I don't bargain with her price of what equals five dollars. She agrees to sell the armband if we give her a lift to her village.

***

We stop at the village of Myangayanga to chat with a University of New Mexico anthropologist here to study the Matengo people. It's hard to tell if he's engaged in a serious project or is enjoying the native beer. Twenty miles on we stop at Kigonsera mission to buy vegetables. When we enter the grounds, I feel as though I've walked into the manicured garden of a medieval castle. In haste I select:

6 lbs. beets

5 lbs carrots

3 lbs. tomatoes

2 bunches parsley

4 heads lettuce

6 cabbages

1 cauliflower

4 onions

15 lemons

20 oranges

a stalk of bananas

My bill comes to about $1.72.

The six cabbages come as a bonus pushing me to make sauerkraut, beet pickles and a big pot of vegetable soup. Saidi brings us more tomatoes, which I'll cook up for ketchup. I boil seedy raspberries I find near a vacant house at the school for jelly and discover mulberry trees I'll be watching. I also learn to stew sliced green papaya with lemon juice and cinnamon as a substitute for apples.

Ketchup

5 pounds fresh tomatoes cooked, pureed and strained
(or 1 28-ounce can crushed tomatoes in tomato
puree, seeds strained out.)
2 tablespoons finely grated onion
1 large clove garlic crushed or minced
2 inches broken cinnamon stick
(or ½ teaspoon ground cinnamon)
10 whole cloves (or ¼ teaspoon ground cloves)
2 allspice berries (or ¼ teaspoon ground allspice)
pinch of crushed red chili or cayenne
1 teaspoon salt
½ cup each sugar and cider vinegar

1. Bring the tomato puree to a simmer. (Add 2-3 cups water to canned crushed tomatoes.) Add the remaining ingredients. (Tie the whole spices in a cheesecloth bag or be prepared to strain the completed ketchup.)

2. Simmer slowly until reduced and thickened. Stir from time to time to prevent burning.

3. Ladle into warm, scalded jam jars and seal while hot or cool, cap and store in fridge.

My sauerkraut reminds me of what my grandma Lapp used to make. I'm careful about scalding the covering cloth every day. Here in the southern highlands the kraut takes only twelve days to ferment instead of five or six weeks in an American autumn. The closest thing we find for wieners to go with it is a little tin of Vienna sausages.

Sauerkraut

    4 pounds garden fresh green cabbage

    9 teaspoons Kosher salt

1. Scald a one-gallon plastic bucket or crock. Gather a clean cotton cloth or plastic wrap and find a saucer and a heavy weight such as a large, clean stone.

2. Shred the cabbage into a large bowl and mix in the salt.

3. Pack the salted cabbage into the bucket or crock pressing it down with your clean fists until it exudes water that covers the top.

4. Cover the top of the cabbage with cloth or plastic wrap and press it down with a saucer. Place a heavy weight such as the stone in a clean plastic bag or a quart jar filled with water on top of the saucer. This will keep the cabbage submerged in it's own liquid.

5. Set the bucket aside in a cool basement or garage to ferment. Check it from time to time to insure a clean smelling, light colored fermentation. Scald the cloth often to prevent molding or keep plastic wrap pushed to the edges of the bucket. Discard kraut if any mold or darkening or off odor develops.

6. In a cool garage, the kraut will be ready in six to eight weeks.

* * *

This afternoon I give Bob a haircut. He insists that I do it behind the storehouse, so no one will see us. Built at the corner of our back garden plot, the storehouse, called simply "the store," is a one-room concrete cubical painted the same cream yellow as our house, complete with hook-ups for a toilet and running water. The stores at the teachers' houses are intended as houseboys' quarters, but no one at our school has live-in help, so servants' quarters become storage sheds.

I silently thank my father for teaching me two things I had no idea I was learning. I observed dozens of haircuts he gave my brothers, qualifying me to scissor Bob's mop with precision. I also studied how he butchered November's venison, and now I cut rough hunks of beef into steaks or stewing cubes, beat out flattened scallops for stuffing, and grind bits for hamburger.

***

It's dry now in late September. We hike over crackly grass past trees with reddish curled leaves. We eye Africans hoeing their river-bed plots. They grasp the short-handled *jembe* (wide hoe) with both hands, swinging it above their heads and plunging it into the earth. We wander among banana plants that skirt a pineapple field beside a stream. I pick wild flowers for a bouquet and listen to birdcalls.

I'm trying to culture cottage cheese from reconstituted powdered milk left in a glass jar covered with cheesecloth. After three days on a pantry shelf, it's begun to clabber.

***

I spend the afternoon watching an Indian man prepare curry. Once in a while Chukla, our local bank manager, comes by to cook for our neighbors, Rich and Vic, and they've included us. I'm learning that real curries are seasoned with a mixture of spices rather than curry powder. Chukla flavors his chicken curry with onion, garlic, chili, turmeric, cinnamon, cloves, tomatoes and coriander leaves. He makes *poories*, deep-fried unleavened breads. He eats everything neatly with his fingers; Bob opts for a fork. Chukla tells us our fingers bring the warm softness of the food directly to our lips without the intrusion of a cold metal fork.

***

Saidi directs us to his wedding after noon on Saturday. He is Moslem, but this will be a traditional African village event, and he's tickled about how enthusiastic we are to take pictures. We drive to the bride's home with Rich and Vic.

We're ushered into a room barely large enough for a card table and four wooden straight-backed chairs. Limp old calendars, government posters and magazine advertisements droop from cello tape on whitewashed walls. Ceiling beams support bamboo rods and burlap under grass thatch. Scuffed linoleum covers a dirt floor. In one corner atop a chest of drawers a battered transistor radio and a wind-up desk clock catch my eye. After waiting half an hour, we're served tall glasses of *togwa,* a thick, slightly sour "sweet" beer not as potent as native *pombe.*

When it's time for the ceremony, a teenaged boy leads us to a thatched shelter surrounded by mud-plastered houses. We sit enveloped in clouds of incense at the edge of thirty bamboo-mat-seated shoeless African men chanting from the Koran. We see no women, not even the bride, throughout the proceedings. The ceremony is a men's affair. I feel conspicuous.

In the center of the gathering, smoke curls from a brazier next to a shallow wok into which men toss coins. Saidi sits beside the incense while an older villager mutters Swahili phrases followed by solemn responses from Saidi and the elders. After quite a bit of this give and take, Saidi rises and walks off. Soon shrill wailing emerges from a house where the women have gathered, announcing the ceremony's end. Another man then gets to his feet, strides through the seated group, distributing copies of the Koran, and monotone chants continue for nearly an hour.

Once again we are ushered toward the little sitting room. A dignified gent leads us to the table, brings in food and leaves us. This is our first taste of real African food cooked in black clay pots over open fires. We eat from a tray mounded with *ugali,* boiled rice, and chunks of spicy goat skewered on sticks, sprinkled with chili and roasted over coals—alongside bowls of stewed fatty, tender chunks of beef simmered in a thin gravy seasoned with tomato, onion and curry powder.

After lunch we go back outside to wait for the bride. We glimpse her long enough to snap a picture of the newlyweds. Saidi sports a white tunic over light blue trousers, an oversized brown and white striped summer-weight suit coat and a white skullcap. The bride appears to be a teenager; we're told she's sixteen and so shy she never lifts her head except once to peek out from under her traditional red and black headscarf. She wears red and black slip-on shoes, a Western-style red and green flowered dress, along with a bandana tied Aunt Jemima fashion, under her poncho-sized scarf. She pauses for a photo, then scurries back inside.

Saidi tells us his bride's family will bring her to his house later when everyone gathers for dancing. I suggest that Saidi bring his wife to our place for tea once she's settled. "Oh, what day should it be?" he asks.

As we return to the school, we notice brush fires smoking near our house. Tanganyikans burn their land to prepare for the next season's planting. These fires often go wild, and this one has circled our walls and charred the bits of grass and low shrubs in our yard. We'll be surrounded by blackened stubble till December.

***

Tuesday I invite Saidi for lunch. Bob and I want to talk about the wedding and hope Saidi will enjoy some American food. I've made buns and serve hamburgers with carrot sticks. These will be easy for him to eat with his hands. We include ketchup, lettuce and tomato—no pickles yet.

For dessert I've prepared chocolate pudding with sliced bananas and orange cookies. Saidi is intrigued with the orange flavor baked into a cookie. After lunch we show him snapshots of our Colorado wedding. He peers at them for a long time and is baffled by my white dress and the tiered wedding cake. We hand him two photos to take home to show his wife—and no doubt the whole village! For a wedding gift we've bought him a flashlight; this pleases him, especially after the many times he's asked, "Will you borrow me your torch?"

OCTOBER 1963

We still have our pet chicken, but I just cooked my first Tanganyikan poulet. I bought it for forty-nine cents and thought it was young enough to be tender, but I needed a hatchet to cut it up. Bob hoped for fried chicken, but I had to pressure-cook the meat first, then fry it slowly for an hour; it was still rubbery.

* * *

One day, a PWD truck drives up. Two *fundies* (craftsmen) jump out with our front-room window. We now have a grand view across our dining table to the great outdoors. The sky is sometimes deep azure scattered with puffy clouds; other times it's gray, streaked with darkness. Red hills roll to our doorstep. Most of the larger trees in the forest that begins at the edge of our yard are wild mangos, their limbs thick with oval leaves. Branches arch into deep-green umbrellas, while low brushy foliage reminds us of scrub oak on Grand Mesa. Scattered taller trees look like Chinese Elms, while others have large waxy leaves. Amid these trees wild grasses cover every patch of dirt. At summer's end when the grass is shoulder high, villagers cut it for roof thatch.

At lunchtime we study crows diving around the trees like trapeze performers. These birds about the size of pheasants have duck-bill-length beaks and elegant white vests. Mornings, they strut and caw in our backyard or dance on our tin roof.

***

Chukla drives out for dinner when he gets news of his transfer to a bank branch in Dar. He's ready to complete his bush assignment, gives us pointers about our December safari and asks us to visit his family in the city. He's Hindu and does not eat beef, so I offer a vegetarian supper with tomato-stewed beans, currant-nut-and-rice stuffed cabbage and halva.

***

I've busied myself canning and preserving; we'll face months when fresh fruit will be scare, and I don't want to spend fifty cents for a one-cup-sized can of imported peaches or plums. Our vegetables are also on-again off-again. For weeks sometimes all we can get are green beans or cucumbers. Then there may be only carrots or peas. Now that I have jar lids, I've canned pickles and soup. Cooking in quantity helps us save on bottled gas. I never indulge in heating the oven unless I'm baking bread and cookies and perhaps a pie for dinner.

***

Bob has had a miserable cold and sore throat for four days, but he finally got a wallop of penicillin yesterday. The doctor at the local hospital gave him a bag of vitamin/antibiotic capsules like the stuff was candy. My ears are plugged and have been ever since our flight from the States. I keep hearing an echo in my head when I breathe or talk.

***

An elderly man in tatters carries a stalk of cooking bananas past our house. I run outside and stop him, asking if he'll bring me sweet bananas. The next morning he arrives with a stalk of maybe a hundred emerald-green bananas. I don't need so many, but he says he's destitute and after we haggle I buy the stalk for forty-two cents. Lo and behold, he comes back the next morning with another stalk of green bananas. Unwilling to take no for an answer, he remains on our doorstep. We round up a schoolboy to explain that we can't use two hundred bananas, but he continues to plead so pitifully that we now have two stalks of bananas hanging in our closet.

* * *

Saturday night we host a dinner for two English couples in town. Both are about our age and work here on government assignments. Arn is the regional secretary, and Al a civil engineer. I chuckle at the way these Brits dress. The rail-thin Arn arrives in an old heavy 1950's charcoal tweed double-breasted suit, while Al wins out in his clown-like checkered suit with a brown and yellow checked shirt and bright yellow tie. I'm perplexed about what to serve since all the British food I've tasted has been flavorless. They enjoy a Bavarian cabbage soup, Swiss steak with Greek-style green beans, Parker House rolls and orange cake. No one leaves a morsel.

* * *

Sunday we drive to Saidi's *shamba* for vegetables. We pass several villages till the road is too narrow for Zelda. Baskets in hand, we hike to the riverside garden plot. We buy tiny new potatoes, green beans, Swiss chard, carrots, onions, and of course a cabbage. Saidi says he works this plot with his father who also owns a second *shamba* planted with coffee, sugar cane and pineapple. He explains that each plot belongs to someone and is passed from the father to the eldest son. Still, we usually see only women and children working the *shambas.*

***

A woman and three children file singly past our house. She's wrapped in a yellow-trimmed green cloth, a *kanga,* from armpits to shins as I would pull a bath towel around myself, tucking it above the bust. Her hair's fashioned in rows of nut-sized twisted knots, and she's showing off an orange plastic bauble necklace. A girl of six or seven follows, clad in a similar dusty-orange cloth. A little boy in muddy shorts and a blue pullover strides ahead of a toddler gowned in a man's shirt with ripped off sleeves and trailing shirttail. This path in front of our window leads from riverside shambas to nearby settlements, and we regularly see women hauling stalks of bananas or fifty-pound loads of firewood on their heads, while a man may pass with a folded umbrella or a tin teakettle balanced atop his hat.

Over the bed I spread out the kanga I bought in Pardan's last week. This rectangular cotton cloth makes up the basic female wardrobe in the bush country. It's a generous yard wide and a bit more than two yards long. Each has a wide border print, a center design emblem and a scripted slogan or proverb. Mine says *Ndugu Kwa Ndugu Umsitupane,* roughly meaning "brother with brother we stand together." The *kanga* becomes a dress, a skirt, a baby sling, a head wrap or a blanket.

***

This morning we learn our acting headmaster Mbenna's two-year-old son died last night. No one can tell us the specific cause of his death. He'd walked though hot ashes and burned his feet a couple of weeks ago. Bob is smitten; he remembers seeing the mother and child last week at the local hospital where the boy was treated, bandaged and given antibiotics. Infection set in. Yesterday Mbenna took his child to Peramiho mission hospital and found it filled to capacity. He was told to bring his son back the following day, but that evening the child died. We're told the funeral will be at two this afternoon.

Suddenly before eleven this morning Bob dashes in saying the funeral is going on right now, and we must leave at once. I'm wearing an old housedress and bobby sox, but there's no time to change. I grab a scarf; we jump into Zelda and join the procession of five faculty cars, the school truck and two Land Rovers transporting the bereaved family. Clouds of dust churn from the rutted road as we make our way to the Matagoro Mission Church.

At the funeral the strangest part for us is the keening or "wailing for the dead." The father and mother appear somber and quiet, while older family members sit grieving with high-pitched cries alternating between lifted phrases of *aahs* and wavering *woos.* They began the lament last evening and they'll continue all day. For an important official or an elder, the crying may go on as long as three days. For a child one day is customary. Rather than simply giving vent to sorrow, the wailing frees the survivors from any connection with witchcraft in the death. The longer and louder the crying persists, the more relieved the survivors are from any guilt associated with the death.

As the crowd enters the church, some Africans fall to the floor, prostrate, shrieking. During the litany before burial the wailing subsides to soft choking sounds. The child's body has been placed in a wooden casket covered with a black cloth. A garland of wild flowers tops a crude white cross, sewn in the center of the cloth. After the brief Latin liturgy we all proceed to the graveyard for a few more prayers before the casket is lowered into a freshly dug pit.

As the group disperses, the wailing resumes, louder than ever. The father stands beside the grave with one of his daughters. The barefoot mother waits behind, her head hidden in a green and white shawl. We stand on the slope and gaze across dry grass, scrub brush and mango trees to the red hills at the base of Matagoro Mountain.

***

We buy two more hens, and our three chickens now give us a couple of eggs a day. Not only are they paying for themselves, but we can buy their week's feed for what we would have to spend for two fresh eggs. We're surprised to find the hens have chosen to nest in the unused porcelain toilet bowl of the unfinished latrine in the empty store or servant's room behind the house. Bob built a straw nest in a wooden box, but the hens went their own way. We've added a soft cloth at the base of the bowl to hold the eggs in place.

***

Our Thanksgiving dinner for fellow Americans will have to be mid-November, since everyone will be away by November 21 for term break. Early on I plan for mincemeat and purchase four expensive, sad apples from the weekly Mbeya food shipment, a cooperative effort organized by a few local women. To supplement the apples I use green papaya. For suet I save some rare scraps of fat from the market beef. The town shops sell raisins and for citron I use homemade candied orange peel. I mix a cup of orange juice with a tablespoon of vinegar for cider. A friend in town sells me a tot of brandy. I seal the cooked spiced fruit mixture in jars following a colonial method I found in an old English cookbook: I top the jar with a circle of paper cut to fit like a lid and rubbed with cooking oil. Over the oiled paper lid I brush two larger circles of tissue paper with egg white and press the egg white slicked paper tightly to the jar's neck. The next morning the paper is dry and hard. I hope the mincemeat keeps for three weeks.

***

Bob and I have been craving pizza. We find a tiny tin of anchovies in a local *duka* and order pork sausage plus plain cheddar cheese from Mbeya; I stretch the pork with ground beef, and simmer a zesty tomato sauce. The crust comes from Saturday's batch of bread, and we demolish the whole cookie-sheet of pizza in one supper.

Basic Bread

For toast, sandwiches or buns, a standard household loaf.

> 16 fl oz. or 2 cups of water (or 1 cup water plus 1 cup
> milk, or 2 cups water plus ⅓ cup powdered milk)
> 2 ¼ teaspoons active dry yeast (1 packet)
> pinch powdered ginger
> 1 tablespoon sugar or honey
> 2 tablespoons wheat germ (optional)
> ½ oz. (1 tablespoon) butter or oil
> 22 oz. bread flour (approximately 4 ½ cups)
> (or mix 17 oz. white bread flour with 5 oz.
> whole-wheat flour)
> 2 teaspoons sea salt

1. Heat the water or milk and water to lukewarm. Pour in mixing bowl. Sprinkle over yeast and ginger. Allow yeast to dissolve.

2. Add sugar, wheat germ, butter or oil and flour. Stir with rubber spatula just to moisten flour. Sprinkle over salt. Cover and rest dough 20 minutes.

3. Knead on a dough hook or by hand for 8-10 minutes or until satiny.

4. Cover with tight lid or plastic wrap and allow to rise until light and double in volume, 1 ½ to 2 hours. Gently deflate dough, folding edges into the center. Invert dough ball, recover and let rise until double again, 30-45 minutes.

5. Shape dough into two medium, 1 very large, or 1 large plus 4 buns and place in greased tins. Cover with a damp tea towel and let rise until light, about an hour depending on the warmth of the room.

6. Preheat oven to 425° F. Slash the loaf lengthwise with a straight-edged razor blade. Mist with water from a spray bottle. Bake the loaves from 25 to 40 minutes depending on size or until golden brown and until they sound hollow when knocked with a fist. Bake buns 18 minutes or until nicely colored.

***

Saidi brought in a basketful of scarce carrots the other day. They tend to get soft if not used right away, and we don't yet have refrigeration except for the butter and cream I keep next door. I recall how we used to dig trenches for root vegetables before winter and think of trenching the carrots in our soft garden soil. We're watering to keep the ground moist, and Saidi's carrots remain crisp.

***

Bob reads a letter from a student:

Dear Sir,

With great honor I politely invite you to attend our meeting of the English Speaking Society, senior section, which will be held in the school hall on 10th October, 1963. Our society will have "Brain Trust" as the topic. So please, sir, I assure you that your presence during the meeting will very much accumulate the pleasure in the hearts of our members. The meeting will start at 7:30 PM.

Yours faithfully,
Matthew

***

It's beginning to get warmer. We've taken the last blanket off our bed. There's still a cool breeze in the morning and by keeping the windows closed, the cement plastered walls hold coolness in through midday, but by afternoon, butter has melted and fresh lettuce is wilted. We're still waiting for a fridge.

NOVEMBER 1963

This morning in the school office after having completed three correspondence courses, I write out the final exam for my last class as an undergraduate. We rush the special envelope to the town post office where it's officially sealed with wax. If the mail doesn't fail, I'll be a college graduate as of December 6th. We plan to be in Nairobi so we'll celebrate with ICE CREAM. Once I have my degree, I'll hope to join the school staff.

***

Peanuts cost "peanuts" here. We buy four and a half pounds of shelled "ground nuts" (as they're called) for thirty-five cents. An Indian woman taught me how to roast peanuts in sand:

Roasting Fresh Peanuts In Sand

1. Gather some clean river sand, wash it, drain and spread over a flat tray and place it in the sun to dry.

2. Heat the sand in a heavy pot, such as the base of the four-quart pressure cooker.

3. Dump in about two cups of shelled peanuts. Keep the pot of sand over medium low heat for 15-20 minutes and stir the nuts from time to time with a long wooden spoon. After 15 minutes test a nut

for doneness every few seconds, remembering they will continue to roast a bit as they cool.

4. At the desired point, pour the nuts and sand into a large sieve held over a cookie sheet.

5. Sift off the sand and spread out the nuts on a tray to cool. When cool enough to touch, rub off the skins, winnow the skins away in the breeze by tossing them upwards in a shallow basket.

6. Make salted nuts by heating them in a teaspoon of peanut oil, adding salt to taste. Prepare peanut butter by running the roasted nuts two or three times through a meat grinder before blending in a little oil and salt.

***

We learn that one of our Indian teachers may be leaving in March, and we're hoping to buy his fridge. This will mean we'll be able to keep lettuce longer than a day.

***

Jane offers to share some graham flour she bought at Peramiho Mission. When I stop by her house for the flour, she introduces me to Maisie, a jolly Irish woman with pulled-back brown hair and the short, strong frame of one who worked as a nurse in Kenya for years before she got married. Her husband, Noel—rhymes with Joel—squat and dark-haired, is our new bank manager replacing Chukla. Maisie, Noel, and their two kids have just arrived. Now that I have this flour from Jane, I'll make graham crackers this afternoon when I bake bread.

48

Graham Crackers

6 oz. (1¼ cups) whole-wheat flour

1 ½ oz. (¼ cup) sugar

¼ teaspoon baking powder

¼ teaspoon baking soda (sieved)

¼ teaspoon salt

2 oz. butter (½ stick)

1 tablespoon honey (optional)

4 to 5 tablespoons milk

1. Stir all the dry ingredients together. Slice cool butter over the flour and rub it in with fingertips to form small flakes. Warm milk to dissolve honey. Sprinkle over 4-5 tablespoons milk, 1 tablespoon at a time, distributing the liquid with a fork. Mix with fingertips to form a soft piecrust like dough adding the last tablespoon of milk only if necessary. Cover and let rest 10 minutes.

2. Roll the ball of dough to a ¼-inch thickness and cut into circles with a biscuit cutter or use a knife to cut squares. Re-roll and cut the scraps. Place crackers on a baking sheet. Prick with a fork and bake at 350º F about 12 minutes or until golden. Hold crackers in turned off oven for crisping. Makes 24 2½-inch crackers.

***

Since Saidi has not been reliable about bringing us produce lately, I set off to see what I can find. I walk to a nearby village and in my minimal Swahili ask if anyone knows someone interested in selling vegetables. A pint-sized boy carries my basket as we head to stream-bed *shambas.* I bargain with a barefoot woman wielding her *jembe* as a baby sleeps in a sling on her back. An hour later after I drop coins into the hands of my young guide and the gardener, I'm back home with green beans, tomatoes and cabbage.

***

Tonight we invite the half-dozen expat bachelor teachers for spaghetti and meatballs, followed by a lime pie that may become my signature dessert. I easily find fresh limes, fresh coconut, tinned condensed milk, and this pie doesn't need expensive fuel for baking.

Lime Snow Pie

Crumb Crust

> 1½ cups graham cracker crumbs (15 squares)
>
> 1 tablespoon sugar
>
> ¼ teaspoon cinnamon
>
> 2 oz. (½ stick) butter, melted
>
> 1 tablespoon honey

Lightly rub few drops flavorless vegetable oil inside 9-inch pie plate. Combine crumbs, sugar, and cinnamon. Mix honey into warm melted butter and combine with crumbs. Press mixture evenly in and up sides of pie plate. Bake crust for 15 minutes in preheated 350°F oven; allow to cool before filling. Baking crust may be skipped; simply chill crumb crust before using. It's good either way.

Filling

> 1 teaspoon grated lime zest
>
> 5 fl. oz. (⅔ cup) freshly squeezed lime juice
>   (increase to 6 fl. oz. (¾ cup) for sharper flavor)
>
> 1½ teaspoons unflavored gelatin
>
> 1 14 oz. tin sweetened condensed milk (not low fat)
>
> 2 organic eggs, rinsed and separated
>
> 6 fl. oz. (¾ cup) heavy cream, whipped (optional)
>
> 1 tablespoon sugar
>
> ¾ cup grated fresh coconut (optional)

1. Dissolve gelatin in ¼ cup lime juice in small cup and allow to stand until it has "sponged" or absorbed liquid. Melt gelatin by placing the cup in saucepan of hot water until gelatin is clear. Hold in warm water.

2. In large mixing bowl, whisk to combine condensed milk, egg yolks, lime zest and remaining lime juice. Gradually beat in melted hot gelatin in lime juice. Beat egg whites with 1 tablespoon sugar until stiff peaks form. Fold egg whites into lime mixture. Fold in whipped cream. Turn lime filling into chilled prepared crumb crust and top with grated fresh coconut if desired. Chill several hours or overnight before serving. Serves 8.

***

The rains have begun. Saturday morning we wake to see the sky filled with low, rolling beds of cloud. When Bob walks out to open the storeroom door for the hens, he steps through a moist spray. Everything feels damp, but we don't get wet even when it sprinkles. These are known as the "mango showers," and they will last a few weeks before heavy rains fall for months. The dry soil is packed so hard that even the lightest breath of moisture in the air is welcome.

***

Early Sunday evening after we've served banana bread and lemon-filled coconut cake for tea with Maisie and Noel, we trudge up to the school. We notice a huge brush fire headed our way. The blaze leaps through tall grass and seems to be closing in on some school buildings. We gather half a dozen schoolboys and our pals next door and, with damp gunnysacks, beat out any flames that get too close. Over the past few weeks we've spotted these grass fires every evening; the locals want to have their land scorched, cleared of weeds and snakes before the big rains.

This evening's program has been organized by the Cooperative Society, a group of schoolboys who've put together a little shop to sell soap, matches and candy. Their modest exercise in grassroots commerce spins off the larger cooperative movement developing throughout Tanganyika. We see village co-ops selling local tobacco, coffee and sugar, and we find the best buys for dry foodstuffs from the Co-op shop in town. After the Society's annual report we're treated to a magic show. A shirtless, turbaned, young Indian man dazzles the school crowd with quick sleights of hand. He juggles huge brass rings, pulls strings of knotted scarves from his ear and swallows flames in the hot African night.

* * *

Close to noon I make my way over to watch Mrs. Mistry, the Indian wife of one of our teachers, prepare *chapatis*. Somewhat like the barley cakes we've read about in the Bible, these thin unleavened breads contain whole-wheat flour, oil and water. In an Indian sari she pads about on bare feet, squats and uses the clean, concrete floor for a kitchen counter. She kneads her dough in a shallow, pizza-type pan. She rolls six-inch pancake-like flat breads with a narrow pin, almost a dowel, on a ten-inch round wooden board, then bakes these dough circles on a black steel disk set over a hot charcoal fire. She flicks the cakes off the disk directly onto a mound of glowing coals on the floor where they puff into balloons. Tipping the puffed *chapatis* from the fire, she spreads each with melted ghee. I'm dying to taste one, but she doesn't offer. I can't ask since she speaks no English, I know no Hindi and I hesitate to use sign language since I haven't brought anything to share.

* * *

Sunday afternoon we stroll up the hill for the customary end-of-term tea party for Zulu Dormitory where Bob is housemaster. In the dining hall we find the bare wood tables decorated with yellow flowers in tin cans. An upside-down aluminum cup and pasted-down paper nametag mark each place. When everyone's seated, the younger schoolboys present themselves as servers. These lower-form boys lack the confidence and swagger of the seniors, but all are dressed in the same pressed khaki shorts and collared white shirts. As they fill teacups, most of the juniors are barefoot and clumsy under the seniors' gaze. First they serve sandwiches made from my bread they've thickly sliced and stuck together with a few dots of jam. They pass around gingersnaps I sent up earlier and make sure every morsel disappears before handing out bananas one at a time. Finally they bring in the candy that most of the young students have never tasted. Many stare at the goodies in their laps before munching them. As one little guy jams a cookie into his mouth, I ask him if he likes it. "Oh, yes, Madam, beyond all expression!"

When I ask if they'd like to visit the States, one boy wants to go to New York to see skyscrapers, another chooses California to see how oranges and lemons grow there. They all want to know what Americans do with maize. I tell them about canning, freezing, grinding into meal, and they're bewildered by the notion of eating corn on the cob. They're certain all milk is tinned or dried. They're astonished when I tell them about dairies and fresh bottled milk available all over America.

After an hour, the speeches commence. When it's time for the head prefect, he makes quite a to-do over the house having a "mother," as well as a "father." He carries on about how their "mother" is a true African parent, for she will not eat till all her children have been served twice. He outdoes himself in expressing thanks for the food we've contributed, while everyone breaks into applause and cheers.

The schoolboys have memorized five- to ten-minute orations. They're not bashful about being called upon to speak. Each fourth-form student has his turn, beginning with something like "As we have worked shoulder to shoulder, hand to hand," or "If we do not meet again on earth, then we shall meet in Heaven."

In unison they rise as Bob and I step from the room, whereupon they rush out the door to shake our hands.

***

We plan to celebrate an early Thanksgiving. We've ordered a leg of lamb from Mbeya. It won't be big enough for all the American staff, so we'll compromise with a big Thanksgiving tea with festive desserts.

On the day our ration of lamb arrives, the guys next door buy a large roasting chicken. They ask me to cook it for a communal dinner. Later two more Yanks join us for mince and pumpkin pie. The homemade mincemeat thrills everyone, and a Tanganyikan squash makes a superb pie.

***

Two days later we bump along twenty miles of washboard roads to visit a couple of Quaker American Field Service volunteers at Mpitimbi. Chickens scratch in the dust beside their rustic mud-walled African house with thatched roof, open doors, and a small reed-fenced courtyard. They are the only white folks who have ever lived in this remote village where everyone carries water a quarter of a mile and families survive on subsistence crops of cassava, maize and bananas. There are no shops closer than Songea.

During the cooler morning hours, Hare advises a team of men about a market square being developed. In a sleeveless loose cotton dress, June walks from house to house helping women with childcare, gently showing them how to bathe their babies. Hare and June have only a motorbike for transport, and in their spartan surroundings, we realize our luxury.

***

When I stop at the mission for graham flour, I purchase a sack of peaches no bigger than walnuts. They're sour, but if we concentrate while we eat them, we imagine the Elbertas we used to pick in Colorado.

* * *

During the second week of November, the rains arrive in full fury. Thursday night brings the first cloudburst. We're visiting another teacher when train-crashing thunder roars, followed by an ear-numbing downpour. We wait nearly an hour for the deluge to lift enough for us to dash twenty-five yards back to our house.

* * *

After the rain this afternoon all at once the air fills with flying ants. The swarm lasts an hour and all but shuts out the sunlight. With gossamer wings, at night, the ants slide under the windowsills and fly toward the light. In the morning I sweep heaps of dead bugs from the living room floor. The ants bother us a few days, though the schoolboys find them a treat. They set a kerosene lamp outside in the dark and as the insects buzz toward the glass-covered flame, the boys clap them inside their hands, pull off the wings and pop the wriggling bodies in their mouths.

* * *

Now that the rains have arrived, we've moved our *kukus* (chickens) into a pen with some hens belonging to another teacher; we've heard they won't lay eggs during rainy season. We feed our hens millet seed, and their egg yolks are deep yellow.

***

As the term ends boys knock at our door asking to borrow money to get home. They sign IOUs to repay us, but we doubt any money will come back. When they stop to say, "Goodbye, thank you for coming to our school, and see you next term," we feel rewarded. Only the fourth-formers or seniors remain at school, scheduled to take their Cambridge exams next week.

***

The flying ants have moved on, but now we have buzzing beetles. At night I want to pull the sheet over my head when I hear them whizzing through our bedroom. The rain also brings out slug-like worms, but most terrifying of all are the spiders. When Bob opens the kitchen pantry door, two eight-legged gray woolies as big as coffee can lids rise onto their toes, ready to spring. He bashes them with a skillet.

***

The rain has stopped. Black clouds billow away while gray-white cushions sail across a golden sky toward dusk. Spears of light spin from the plunging sun. For the first time I observe the never-ending circular panorama of the earth as though I were turning on a lily pad in the middle of a pond. No building stands in the way of the horizon as the evening sky settles like a giant dome.

***

A boy in dirty white shorts knocks at the door and hands me a note from Saidi: "Many greetings to you" preface his note informing us his uncle—anyone from his grandfather to a distant cousin—has died and he needs to travel to Dar at once. I have a huge load of wash that must be done, all by hand in the bathtub, and everything must be pressed using a charcoal heated iron. We've been good to Saidi, and I feel a bit put out.

Our neighbors suggest a schoolboy, Nesibu, who lives nearby and can work during the winter school holiday. Later that morning Bob sees him in town and asks him to come by. We hire Nesibu for the week. But early Tuesday morning, in my curlers and pink hairnet when I run to answer a knock at the door, both Nesibu and Saidi stand outside. Nesibu is now in charge of washing socks while Saidi turns up soil for a garden. Nesibu scrubs our shirts white and irons them perfectly. I ask him to return tomorrow to wax the living room tile. Meanwhile Saidi hauls manure from the school barn and prepares two twenty-foot rows for planting. If he comes back tomorrow, we'll have two more rows and can plant seeds before we leave next week.

***

Bob finishes correcting final exams and changes the oil in the car before he has it greased in town. We'll safari out tomorrow and won't be back till early January. We'll carry gallon jugs of gas, sleeping bags and plenty of boiled water. I fill two of the five-pound powdered milk tins with peanut butter cookies and graham crackers for snacks with bananas. I wrap spice cakes, coconut wafers and orange hermits to leave with friends along the way. We'll be packed tightly but plan to make room for one schoolboy who needs a lift to Njombe.

If we get stuck on muddy roads, we're hoping there'll be PWD workers along the roads to help. By seven a.m. tomorrow we plan to be headed toward Kenya and as far as the Ruwenzori Mountains in Uganda. Just two or three days to ICE CREAM!

***

Odom, a husky schoolboy knocks at our door about 6:30, and the three of us leave the mud puddles of Songea in a cloud of mist following a rainy night. The haze so densely covers the hills we can't see the trees that nearly touch our front porch. The umbrella branches and grasses look jungle-like. Birds dart ahead of us; one is summer-squash yellow with charcoal wings and a red band at its throat. Beyond the eroding humped hills surrounding Songea we drive atop woodless crests, making our way up the Lukumburu escarpment. Although we slither and skid, I hold my breath as Bob keeps his foot on the accelerator. We slide through waves of mud and make record time, barreling through one hundred eighty two miles to Njombe in five hours.

***

On the morning of November 23 we sit at a white linen-covered table in the dining room at Iringa's White Horse Inn and stare into saucers of grapefruit. The seedy white centers have been neatly cored and heaped with sugar. As we're spooning the segments, the Greek hotel proprietor rushes to our table. He tells us the news he's just heard on his ham radio. Napkins in hand, we follow him into his office, and in disbelief, thousands of miles from home, listen to the announcement that our president has been assassinated

***

We push on toward Dodoma, and join the Great North Road to Arusha. In one day we motor past sun-beaten plains, sand-swept valleys and lush forests. Near Arusha the landscape stretches into a green carpet dotted with wide-leaved banana plants and immense hardwoods. We drive by sisal fields, where giant tractors creep over plantations. The plains feed into vast grasslands before the rising pyramid of Mount Meru. Three *twiga* (giraffes) graze ahead, our first sighting of big game.

By late afternoon we stop at a hotel in Arusha, a fair-sized town with high-rise buildings and three movie theaters. In the city center bead-bejeweled Masai wander among Asians and Europeans. We notice a snack stand selling hamburgers, hot dogs and doughnuts, but no ICE CREAM.

***

Sunday afternoon we step quietly beneath the tolling bell tower of the Evangelical Lutheran Church for a memorial service for President Kennedy. Heavy silence fills the packed stuccoed sanctuary where we stand arm to arm black, white, tan—people of the world. The air echoes with Bach and "Lord, have mercy." We return to the African sun with eyes downcast and learn the suspected assassin has been shot.

***

We purchase food for the three days we hope to spend in Serengeti Game Park, and after lunch Monday we set out for Ngorongoro Crater. Along the way we see ostriches taller and larger than workhorses as eagles and buzzards circle overhead.

We glimpse regal Masai herding flocks of goats and cattle. The men rub their skin with earth, which makes it reddish brown and entwine beads in their thick braided hair. They drape brown cloth toga-like from one hip to a tie at the opposite shoulder; the breeze fans their bare bottoms. The plainer Masai women closely crop their hair, wear wide beaded collar necklaces in strong primary colors and wrap themselves in black or red cloth. Most of the men wave to us in passing.

When Bob jumps out to snap a picture of Mount Meru, a grinning African dashes from his roadside hut, engaging us in elementary Swahili, hoping we'll pay him for a photograph. We stop at a village to buy bananas and continue to climb to Ngorongoro crater's rim above 10,000 feet.

**

As cold and rainy as it is outside, fireplaces warm the main Ngorongoro lodge. We sit on Danish modern chairs in the glass-walled dining room. In the middle of dinner the waiters call "Buffalo!" and everyone scrambles to the windows to peer at three massive ox-like cows within a hand's reach. As we sip coffee by the lodge fire, we chat in halting French with an elderly Swiss couple; they invite us to join them in their touring Land Rover the next day. We're grateful for their offer. On the walk back to our motel-like room we wonder if we'll meet lions on the trail.

Early the next morning, we join our Swiss friends and descend from the rocky rim into the crater, the world's largest volcanic caldera. We're all eager to explore the crater floor that covers over one hundred square miles—that's more than three times the size of the city of Grand Junction, Colorado. After half an hour down the steep escarpment taking us two thousand feet below the rim, we sail along a carpet of dewy meadow grass. The crater abounds with herds of zebra, wildebeest and gazelle. Both the larger Grant gazelle and the smaller Thompson wear a delicate fawn coat and a white vest. They have pointed black horns, black eye lines and a narrow black stripe along their sides. The wildebeest look fierce and funny with the head of a moose, horns of a shorthorn steer, front quarters of an American bison and rear of a small cow. We find deer-like waterbuck, hartebeest, eland and topes. The rarest animal we see is a mammoth black rhino with a curved double horn, whose elephant-type paws hold up tons of squatty, hog-thick flesh. As we stare out the roof of the Rover, the rhino appears too lazy to move. When we near the lake that covers a large part of the crater base, our African guide hands out boots and suggests we wade through mud to the lake's edge to watch hippos. We hear their snorts but no heads surface, since they seldom come out of the water during the day. Although we comb the crater, we don't glimpse a lion.

Cranes and herons wade in another side of the lake nestled in the crater's floor. We study a family of ostriches with two chicks. The red-necked black male is more than two hundred pounds heavier than the gray-brown female. We notice a scattering of foxes, jackals, hyenas. Patches of pink or white wild petunias, yellow daisies, sweet peas and pink shooting star lilies dot the crater's lawn floor. Arching acacia trees and humpy oaks offer shade while Masai herd livestock inside the crater as they have for centuries.

As we climb out of the caldera, our driver struggles to shift into a low gear. The Rover slips backwards until both the driver and our guide tug on the hand break stopping the Rover within inches of the cliff's edge.

***

Early the next morning we take on a new passenger. A middle-aged merchant seaman from Illinois hitches a ride to Serengeti. Short and muscular, with mustache and a squint, he has the don't-mess-with-me-I've-seen-it-all look. Last September he traveled through Europe and the Middle East, followed patches of the Great North Road from Egypt to Cape Town. He sold his car in South Africa and returned to East Africa where he'll hire on as a ship's engine man in the port city of Mombassa. We offer him a lift, providing he'll help dig us out if we get stuck.

***

We plot our course northwest along a hazardous road thirty-eight miles toward Olduvai Gorge, then sixty miles on to Serengeti. Determined to see the anthropological dig at Olduvai, we take the risky trail since it's the only access at this time of year. We drive alongside the deeply rutted main road and shoot through two knee-deep rivers till we reach the site sponsored by *National Geographic* magazine.

A young Kenyan anthropologist shows us around the digs. With evangelistic zeal, he tells us of the July day three years ago when Louis Leakey lay feverish in camp. His wife Mary set out to walk their Dalmations, and discovered part of the skull of the earliest known cave person. Paleoanthropology hit the international news. Four of us stand under the desert sun in this vast dry gulch once pastureland and once the home of our earliest ancestors. We circle the low thatch-covered mound where Zinjanthropus lay for almost two million years.

***

On the track toward Serengeti an adjacent grassy field looks better than the road, so we drive alongside the road till we slam into a drainage ditch where we work against the clock to hoist the rear end out of the mire. Bob and our passenger, Sharp, jack up the wheels, as we wedge rocks underneath them. After two frantic hours we roll Zelda out of the ditch, only to find a flat tire. Still in a rush, the men replace the flat with a spare, and we slide past the park gates minutes before they're locked for the night. As Americans roast Thanksgiving turkeys, we have a camp supper of Spam and tinned beans.

***

The next day we hire a guide and rove the park in our VW. When we get stuck in a marsh, Bob, Sharp and our guide dig us out while I imagine leopards lurking in the branches overhead. About eleven o'clock the camp Rover ahead spots a pride of lions feasting on last night's kill. We leave the main road and follow their grass trail cross-country to find the lions resting under an acacia tree. Too lazy and well fed to mind being watched, they loll on the grass. We make sure the car windows and doors are shut and leave the engine running so the smell of petrol muffles our scent; we button our lips and pull closer. The lithe cats with golden coats shine in the morning sun. This pride of sixteen lions includes a heavy-maned male, three females and twelve cubs. Two females rip flesh from a zebra's carcass while the male rests, panting, and the cubs nip and chase one another in the shade; jackals circle and vultures careen overhead.

***

The Serengeti appears endless. Herds roam everywhere; we could drive across this savanna for days without seeing another car.

We say goodbye to Sharp, who will hitch another ride. I rouse the staff boy who holds the keys to the communal kitchen where I boil water for tea and scramble eggs. Two cheetahs cross our path as we inch out of the park. For five and a half morning hours we gun it through nine knee-deep rivers along a hundred and thirty miles to Lake Manyara.

***

We lounge in Lake Manyara Hotel's swimming pool and manicured gardens. We wait in cliff-perched lookout shelters for signs of wildlife at the foot of the Rift Valley mountains and watch flocks of dark pink flamingos land with a splat in the black mud at the lake's edge.

From Lake Manyara we cross into Kenya, game-parking at the vast Tsavo Reserve. In the afternoon we catch yawns from lolling hippos and crocs at Mzima Springs on the western edge of the park, and check in at the cabin office. Animal-spotting-cocky, we drive out alone toward evening on a dusty park trail. All at once the brush seems to explode as a gigantic male elephant erupts, trumpeting, ears flapping, tusks slashing the air directly ahead of us. Bob slams the car into reverse, burns rubber backwards and dust flies.

December 1963

When we reach the outskirts of Nairobi, crowds startle us. If traffic is terrifying, the taste of cold, pasteurized milk is wondrous. Everywhere there's poverty, wealth, confusion. Nairobi's mobs, all one hundred and sixty thousand people, press me to buy.

Nairobi, Nairobi, Nairobi, you teem with huger masses than ever. Three days from now your celebration for Kenya's independence begins. Your buildings are draped in red, black and green. Giant shields flanked by crossed spears loom at every traffic circle. Double-decker buses, taxis and bicycles clog the avenues, while pedestrians jaywalk helter-skelter.

We try to get stadium tickets for the flag-raising ceremony, only to be sent on a goose chase from one non-existent office to another—until an Englishman who points out that we're the wrong color advises us to give up and be content with watching the event on TV. In the afternoon we elbow our way through the crowd close to the highway's edge on the official route. Just ten feet ahead of us, waving from open convertibles, are Prime Minister Jomo Kenyatta and Prince Philip, Duke of Edinburgh. The whole city pulses with shouts of *Harambee* (Let us pull together), Kenyatta's rallying cry.

***

We find lodgings at the Thika Road House, a hostel-type hotel—nothing fancy, but it's clean and packed with tourists like ourselves.

Here at Thika we've met our New York housemates, Bill and Kat who were posted mid-country in Kenya. Little Chris has grown into a beanpole of a toddler, and Kat is expecting another baby in April. We've planned to go out for a steak dinner with them this evening, but Bob and Bill are both struggling with diarrhea, so we'll stay put.

***

We connect with other TEAers on holiday in Nairobi. Some city-posted teachers worry about robberies, and one couple has had their car stolen. Friends in Moshi move all valuables into their bedroom at night and hang saucepans on their door handles as burglar alarms. We may be isolated in Songea, but we don't worry about safety. A family at a Nairobi school invites nearly thirty TEAers for a picnic where we regroup with friends from summer's training. Afterwards we go to an evening performance featuring Harry Belafonte and Miriam Makeba. We're surprised to learn that although Belafonte has long worked to advance the cause of African people and American Negroes, this is his first visit to Africa.

***

By Wednesday, December 12, 1963, the countries of East Africa will be independent nations. On Monday the 10th *Uhuru* (independence) comes to the island of Zanzibar, and at midnight on December 11th, the Union Jack comes down for the last time while the new Kenyan flag is raised at Nairobi's Independence Stadium. Tanganyika gained independence in '61 and Uganda in '62.

***

We celebrate my graduation with a gala dinner at Alan Bobbie's Bistro, a posh French eatery, in Nairobi. I order asparagus, duck á l'orange, and French chocolate ice cream pressed between layers of hazelnut cake that makes me dream of Parisian patisserie.

After dinner we sit in on a dance concert where Ethiopian musicians play wooden flutes, clarinet-like horns, drums and stringed viols. The melodies sound unearthly at first, but after a while we're drawn in. The women skip around in white slippers, filmy white knee-length dresses with red and blue embroidery edging and keep white chiffon veils over their heads and shoulders. The men lead forth in heavy sandals, animal skins, feathers and change to prim white suits with embroidered shoulder scarves, and white stage shoes.

***

Having had our fill of Nairobi, we set out for Kampala. It's a numbing, four hundred mile drive, but we make good time and arrive just after four p.m. This part of Uganda is a riot of lush green, with smooth tarmac roads bordering patches of sugar cane and cotton fields. Rather than rainy and dry seasons, Kampala has one season of light rain and one of heavy rain, allowing for two full-crop rotations each year. Now in mid-December, we enjoy the light rains that come and go through the day.

We discover thumb-sized sweet red bananas that taste faintly of vanilla and syrup-oozing golden pineapples. We pass women in puffy sleeved blouses and long skirts with big sashes. We're told Queen Victoria once visited Uganda decked out in this type of dress, which was then adopted in Buganda, the area around Kampala.

Like Rome, Kampala is built on seven rolling green hills. Makerere University buildings fan out over a tropical botanical garden in long three-story square-built rows. The towering Freedom Statue draws our eyes to the child held aloft in the hands of the person emerging from bands of bondage.

We're staying in the apartment of a TEA administrator who left us a key while he's away. After three weeks of hotel food, I'm eager to cook. We walk to an outdoor market for vegetables and fruit. At a meat shop we buy lamb, pork chops, and sausages. This evening I cut my portion of lamb into minuscule pieces to make it last as long as possible. For dessert we indulge in—guess what—ice cream and make hot fudge sundaes with sliced pygmy-bananas.

It's past mid-December, though we see no sign of Christmas except for a string of tinsel in a small store and a packaged plum pudding on a grocery shelf.

At Kampala's National Theatre when the Agency for International-al Development shows an hour-long documentary about President Kennedy's assassination, including Johnson's inaugural address, we see the tragic procession of JFK's funeral. We listen to the clip clops of the horse drawn carriage and watch the black clad cortege. Along with everyone present, we depart in silence—while people all over the world are calling Americans ugly.

***

In the morning there's a knock at the apartment door and—out of the blue—it's Jim and Shirl from Grand Junction. I remember Jim well from high-school days with his rugged cowboy looks and basketball hoopster height. Shirl's blond fringed face is as welcome as the sighting of Mount Garfield in our Colorado desert valley. We exchange holiday greetings and plan to meet at their school in Lushoto on our way to Dar after Christmas.

***

Through waves of dust we push out of sweltering Kampala. We reach Murchison Falls in time for a three-hour float—in nauseating heat, through an infestation of flies—on the legendary Victoria Nile. We sight hippos, crocs and elephants. We sail mid-river below the waterfall where torrents rush through a narrow gap spewing foam on the river and spraying mists into the air. We bake in the afternoon sun till our arms tan and freckle, then return to the park lodge in time for five-o'clock tea. After warm baths, we eye the sunset from the terrace, waiting for dinner.

* * *

Due to heavy rains and closed roads, we've had to alter our plan to visit the Ruwenzori Mountains, home of protected gorillas. Although we had to stop short of our goal, the Hotel Margherita in Kasese, in the foothills of the "Mountains of the Moon," serves the same dinner we've had every night. Thankfully, we both like lamb.

The next day we step out of Zelda to stand inside the upright circle marking the equator. In Queen Elizabeth Park we swelter but don't feel all that far from snow-capped Colorado. We drive through tall grass on park trails where young elephants are the only big game out in the afternoon. Here in southwestern Uganda the roads are dry; rains in this part of the country are two months away. Barely two hundred miles from Kampala, we're in a totally different climate zone.

Sunday we forge through forested hill country over well-paved roads from Queen Elizabeth Park south through Mbarara, then east to Masaka and north back to Kampala. Bob lets me take the wheel for nearly a hundred miles, and I clip along between sixty and seventy. We pass craters, none as large as Ngorongoro, some filled with lakes and others with dense grass and low trees. As we near the capital city we welcome thick tropical foliage after the dry plains of the last two parks. When tea plantations line our route, we stop to snap photos of the workers who shout, *Hapana* (No).

We're warned there will soon be trouble here for whites. Yesterday six Brits were deported for giving a party where an African was sup-

68

posedly ridiculed. The house where the party took place was burned to the ground. The local newspaper predicts more whites will be deported for the incident. There was no evidence of a search for the truth in this matter; there was no trial, no investigation. No warrant was issued to find who set fire to the house.

***

It's Christmas Eve in East Africa. We buy a bouquet of pink and white carnations and a candle for our apartment dining table. We look for small gifts. Bob chooses a bottle of his favorite aftershave, and I pick out a paperback copy of Elizabeth David's *French Country Cooking*.

We shop for Christmas dinner and anticipate our shrimp cocktail, a small roasted chicken with rice and mushroom stuffing, white wine and ice cream with strawberries. I manage to bake a simple yellow cake and cinnamon rolls to share with the English woman who lives next door. Happy Christmas—as they say here in the British tradition.

***

Back in Tanganyika outside Moshi on our way to see Jim and Shirl, we turn onto the Tanga road, and read the sign, "Road impassable after 100 miles." The road looks car-worthy—so we assume the sign was put up some time ago and has not been taken down, like many we've seen. After three hours on a bumpy stretch of a hundred and twenty miles, we come to a rusted steel beam bridge completely washed out alongside a wildly flowing river. We have no choice but to turn around and go back. We drive three hundred miles to nowhere that day. We'll have to give up the stop to see Jim and Shirl.

***

The only other way to Dar is via Dodoma and Morogoro, five hundred and fifty miles, and we wonder if we can make it in one day. We ask the Arusha hotel desk to give us a five-thirty morning call.

When we go to bed that night, it starts to rain. It continues to pour all night. I keep waking and worrying.

We leave Arusha at six a.m. in the rainy dark, with water four inches deep flooding the road. All at once the day brightens, and just as the tarmac ends, the rain lets up. We stop twice for ten-minute breaks and reach Dar towards evening. I try to sleep, but the day's tension won't leave my head, and I feel like I'm still on the road all night. At six-thirty the next morning, we meet our friends, Hans and Joy, at the airport.

* * *

Zanzibar charms the four of us. The scent of cloves is everywhere as we step into the world of Scheherazade. Veiled women skim sylph-like through donkey-cart cobbled lanes, then slip behind massive mahogany doors studded with elephant spikes. Incense wafts from dark shops with hanging bead door curtains. Vendors beckon us in, offer glasses of hot tea and tempt us with small carpets and brass-bound teak chests.

We hire a cab with Hans and Joy to visit Persian ruins where arched stone doorframes stand among wall fragments and piles of lichen-covered rubble. We descend steep stone steps into a dirt-floored slave cave pocked with wood soot. We circle clove estates and stop to buy bags of the reddish brown, nail-shaped spice that perfumes the car with sweet, piney aroma. We linger at a plantation and learn how coconut husk is turned into rope. The hard brown shell is pulverized for laminated boards, and the dried meat becomes copra, used for oils, soaps and margarine. All this is a far cry from my grandmother's coconut layer cake.

We walk barefoot over white sand in a Shangri-la-like cove. We're tempted to strip off our clothes and float in the ocean as we wade in wavelets under coconut palms. We hoped to welcome the New Year under colored lights of the French/Arabic outdoor cafe Pigalle, but after a cozy supper of shrimp and *frites* our adrenaline rush gives out long before midnight. I dream myself to sleep with visions of a silk-sailed dhow carrying me across a river of crystal light into a sea of dew.

January 1964

On New Year's Day we follow narrow old-town streets. We dip in and out of shops, aching to buy an Arab carpet but can't strike a deal. Instead we purchase a square Christmas card–sized wooden box decorated with carved leaf fronds, four tiny silver Turkish coffee spoons and an antique brass tray with a long shallow dipper that reminds us of a giant gong.

***

Back in Dar we camp at Hans and Joy's. Around noon the first day, Joy asks me to boil up a pot of oxtail soup using a dried Knorr packaged mix. When the soup turns lumpy, she directs me to the blender. I've never used a blender. I approach it uneasily and fail to squeeze the lid firmly onto the thin plastic jar. Before I know it, gravy-thick soup spews from the blender, scalding my right hand, wrist and lower arm. I flee screaming into the backyard. Bob grabs my burned arm and plunges it into a sink of cold water, a new burn therapy he'd come across recently in *Time* magazine. In shock, I sob for two hours while Bob drives me to the hospital where I'm bandaged, injected with penicillin, and dismissed with a tube of gooey yellow salve.

By Saturday morning I'm protecting my gauze-covered arm as we finish shopping and feel as though we've bought out the town. We splurge on a case of wine—red and white for drinking, sherry and port for cooking. We come upon a shop with wholesale prices on canned foods. Our Songea friend, Chukla, guides us through the Indian commercial neighborhood where I outfit my cook's wares with a lava rock grinding stone, a brass mortar and a *chapati* board.

We follow Chukla home for dinner. His extended Indian family of nine seems contentedly cramped in a neat-as-a-pin four room apartment. The tiny kitchen has no cabinets or work boards. A few open shelves line one wall next to a little electric stove and a minuscule sink. Women squat or sit on the cement floor while they peel vegetables and sweep the peelings into a corner. Pots simmer over low charcoal braziers; the electric stove is used to boil water. I observe the vegetarian dinner of chili-laced lentils, eggplant fried with onions, steamed rice, fiery coconut chutney plus thick curd (yogurt) and *chapatis*. We feast on a mat-covered floor and lick the spicy oils from our fingers.

Chukla's wife and sisters present me with a hand-woven rust and white sari. They advise me about the undergarments I'll need to sew and show me how to wrap the long cloth about my waist, pleating it in front before tucking it securely and draping the remaining length over my opposite shoulder.

***

The historic long-deserted ghost city of Bagamoyo sits forty miles north of Dar. We park at a mission museum there near the oldest Roman Catholic church in Tanganyika and meet a Dutch Father who shows us around the crumbling stone dwellings of this town established by Arab traders in the thirteenth century as the first port and initial capital of Tanganyika. We walk around moss-patched crumbled stone walls of the city, imagining the trade that must have flourished here hundreds of years ago until Dar with its better harbor commandeered the population southward. At this point the state has no money available for restoration.

***

Road-weary after six weeks, we approach the school late in the afternoon. Our driveway is overgrown, and the grass cucumber-green. In the house cobwebs lace the corners, and the doors are warped from the damp. We expect to see a bounteous vegetable garden in our backyard, but only a few scraggly bean plants and a couple of corn stalks have survived the weevils and slugs. We feel like royalty now able to bathe in our own tub, to sleep in our own bed and to have our own cooked food. Even in Africa—perhaps especially in Africa—there's no place like home.

***

My days as a woman of leisure are over. After talking with the ministry last week, I'll begin teaching French part-time this term and will go on to full-time in April, taking on some English classes after five of our current teachers complete their tours. The ministry refuses to recognize my degree since I did not come into the program under TEA myself. I'll be paid the same as an African teacher who has no university training. That will work out to be about fifty cents an hour—babysitting wages—for class time, with not one penny for preparation and grading papers. Still, I'm eager to get on with it.

***

After our six-week safari across East Africa over daredevil stretches of road, on Thursday we drive to town for supplies. There have been recent heavy rains and the road is rutted. On our return trip we round the familiar blind curve with a steep downhill grade on the one-way track. Both approaching cars forget to lay on the horn, both cars swerve, both to the right and we collide head-on with Bry, a fellow teacher. At the end of our trek, barely two miles from home, Zelda sinks into a crumpled heap. Her left front fender, hood and bumper have taken a direct hit, and her steering wheel is cracked. Except for a bruised knee, Bob is unscathed, but I'm thrown forward; I hit my nose on the windshield and my knees dent the metal dash.

The police cite the damages but don't know how to assess blame for an accident that was no one's fault, considering the blind curve. We wait for Teeteeco, the state bus and trucking company, to tow both cars out to the school.

* * *

Carless and dismayed, at least we can attend to our injuries. My knees swell as big as basketballs and my left foot sprouts an infection. A few days ago I was helpless with my scalded arm. Now I can barely walk.

When we notice the infection developing in my foot, Pillay drives us to Peramiho. A nurse gives me a penicillin injection, dresses my wounds and tells me to return in three days for another shot. Pain blazes through my foot when I put any weight on it. The infection tingles and feels like an open runny sore. I'm weak and sleep five hours in the middle of the day.

This afternoon my foot hurts so bad that I can't stop crying. Our neighbor drives us to the government hospital in the village. We find an African doctor who shoots me up with more penicillin, cleans and redresses my sores, using a vile-smelling yellow solution. I'm well cared for, but as I look around I realize I'd dread having a major operation here under a kerosene lamp with rats scuttling over the tin roof. My dressing burns for half an hour, but it gradually quiets down, throbbing now and then but not turning me inside out with pain.

The next day the pain is so intense I spend hours in bed knocked out with codeine. I'm deathly afraid to take it, but it's all we have. I've been lying down with my foot on a hot water bottle to encourage the foot to drain.

By Thursday I'm hobbling with multicolored knees. We celebrate with our neighbors. Pizza, not penicillin, may be the best medicine! Along with our good cheese and salami from Dar, Rich donates a can of mushrooms he's tucked away. I find a long-lost green pepper from Iringa. Surely tonight's is the grandest pizza in all of Africa, and we top it off with a bottle of Chianti.

***

After my scalded arm and our car crash, we realize we've come to this continent dreadfully ill equipped. We don't have a decent antiseptic in the house. We've brought along a battered Red Cross first-aid book, but it tells nothing about what to do for burns or infections. We have aspirin, Johnson's first-aid cream, insect repellent, Band Aids, but nothing more. With no news about our car, we bum rides from our colleagues.

***

As we recall combing Zanzibar's beaches days ago, we're jolted to hear of the insurrection that bloodied the island on January 12, scarcely a month after independence from Great Britain. A Ugandan immigrant led the underdog natives, armed with axes and spears, in a mutinous riot, overthrowing the ruling sultan. They went on to seize arms from the police, captured the radio station and rallied the poorer African neighborhoods. The sultan fled in his yacht; five thousand Arabs were slaughtered by Africans. In the next few days hundreds of Arabs crowded into dhows and shoved out to sea, while countless Arab treasures were dumped into the Indian Ocean. We'd hoped to return to that idyllic island, but now the picture has darkened.

***

Bob starts school today, and I'll begin Monday with just a few ideas and a couple of pamphlets on elementary French I picked up in Dar.

Despite the mud mess, we enjoy the everyday rain. If it begins just as we're going to bed or sitting down for a meal, we lend an ear as it plinks on our tin roof like a lullaby. Or we wait in silence as it pounds in waves of fury. What a mistake not to bring galoshes or knee-high boots! Every time we step outside, our shoes sink into wet grass even if it's not raining, and we squish around on spongy damp soles all day. We never leave the house without an umbrella, even though it's just a hop next door.

We run the laundry in and out between showers, but clothes never dry till they're ironed—and everything must be pressed under heat to kill possible mango fly eggs. These common insects often lay eggs on clothing outside and their larvae will burrow into our skin. Almost all households here use a charcoal iron. This cast-iron pie-shaped implement is hollow inside. A wooden handle on top tilts back the upper plate to reveal a cavity for charcoal embers ignited in a brazier just outside the kitchen door. Zigzagging vents along the iron's sides allow airflow to keep the charcoal burning white-hot. Water flicked on the ironing surface shows the temperature, and a press cloth protects a delicate shirt from scorch. The wooden kitchen worktable padded with a blanket and towels becomes an ironing board. We end up with ironed socks and panties, as well as towels, sheets and pillowcases.

***

During the rainy season, the plane from Mbeya often can't land on the mud-slick Songea strip. This means no mail, no food shipment, no news from the outside world. This also means our letters can't get out.

A bridge has washed away on the Lindi Road. We hoped for shipments over the Njombe Road, but now that route is impassable as well. Smokers are going bonkers without cigarettes, and there's no petrol to be had. We Europeans depend on houseboys with bicycles and whatever they can scour from the town market. The other day I rode into town with the school truck just before the road closing and stocked up on a supply of sugar and flour, but I continue to crave vegetables. Pillay gives me enough green beans from his garden for two meals.

The gravel path in front of our house has collected water at least an inch deep, and our circular flowerbed is a pond. Close as we are to the equator, it's chilly most of the day. Bob bundles up in wool socks and a heavy sweater. The sky's overcast till afternoon when the sun peeks out briefly.

* * *

At Friday's market I'm lucky to find cabbages, a handful of marble-sized potatoes and a papaya. A schoolboy hefts a bag of coconuts from his home, and I buy five large ones for ten cents apiece. By grating the fresh coconut, spreading it on a cookie sheet and leaving it in a closed oven for a couple of days I get sweet dried coconut flakes.

Three other schoolboys surprise us with gifts from their home-towns. Michael brings us a pound of freshly roasted, ground coffee from a village near Mbeya. (I've made an Austrian chocolate torte for our weekend dessert, which will be delicious with a good cup of coffee.) Michael also presents us with a cloth bundle of white navy-like beans as well as reddish-brown beans that look like pintos. I'm delighted; the only beans I've been able to find here are large black ones that cook up like kidney beans.

Samuel, from the Lake Nyasa area, shows us a wooden cigar-box-sized musical instrument that looks like a small stringless guitar. It's a thumb piano with two sound holes and line of heavy wire "keys"—spokes from an umbrella—secured at the top edge leaving the ends free near the sound holes. I balance the box on both palms and plink the wires with my thumbs.

Masudi, who lives near Mtwara, brings us a sack of cashew nuts still in the shell. To remove the nuts from their shells, they must be warmed over a fire outdoors since nut oil splashes when the kernels burst from their shells. Masudi tells us how these cashews develop at the blossom end of their pear-like fruit and are broken off when the fruit is ripe. The growers eat the ripe cashew pears or ferment them into an alcoholic drink. Masudi will come over one day next month after he has completed his month of Ramadan fasting, and we'll extract the cashew nuts. He warns us that the nuts are poisonous if not prepared right.

Once all his older history students have returned, Bob discusses JFK's assassination. Even though six weeks have passed, some school-boys from distant villages still haven't heard the news. Most students realize that the President supported the United Nations, which they all revere. Some remember Kennedy's praise for their own president, Julius Nyerere, for desiring "equality for everyone." One boy tells Bob, "Sir, Mr. Kennedy sent us you." They recall the test ban treaty, and husky Masudi comments, "Mr. Kennedy believed it was better to talk over disagreements rather than to shoot first."

***

I'm pleased with my French class of twenty third-form boys. Despite their dreadful pronunciation, they try hard to say their *Bonjour's* and *Au revoir's*, and they get a big bang out of learning new words like *jardin* (garden) and *vache* (cow). Last night I helped Bob mark his English compositions; he had his classes write about returning to school after their holidays. Many went without food and lodgings for days as their buses got stuck in the mud or broke down. When they arrived at school, several new students mentioned they were astonished to see electricity, white teachers and sturdy school buildings.

***

Saidi left for Dar at the end of November and still hasn't returned. We doubt he'll come back, since he owes a lot of money here and next door. Lucas works mornings for Pillay and will come by for a couple of hours in the afternoon. He's now energetically digging some fresh garden rows and is quick with house chores. He's so poor he doesn't own a bike, but he's such a good worker that we're letting him stay longer than we planned.

He tells Bob that his primary school chose him as a candidate for secondary school, but without funds he was unable to enroll. Although he wants to learn, he claims he's too old for classes. He's hoping to marry at the end of the year. The price for his bride is four hundred shillings and two goats. The bride price must come out of his pay with which he also supports his parents and younger siblings. Bob offers to loan him a few schoolbooks. Pole-thin and good-natured, always dressed in a clean short-sleeved cotton shirt and dark blue trousers, Lucas works like a trouper. I know he doesn't get enough to eat, so I offer him snacks. He lives five miles away and must leave home on foot early each morning, only to trudge home after five under his umbrella. I wish we could drive him, and I wonder if there is any supper waiting.

***

We've had little news of the uprising in Dar earlier this month. In the wake of the early January rampage on Zanzibar, army mutineers in Dar ransacked part of the city and forced President Nyerere into hiding for two days until a group of British marines brokered a peace. We Americans here at the school receive a telegram from the AID director in Dar, saying all is calm now in the city and we shouldn't worry, but if we have questions, we should feel free to call him. Well, how in the world are we going to call? Drive a full day to Iringa to find a phone? We can send letters and telegrams from the local post office, but anything else would be out of the question. The AID telegram tells us how removed our government officials are from the real Africa, the Africa of the bush.

We hope the American press has not sensationalized the situation. Most Africans in this region aren't aware that anything has happened. Even the schoolboys consider it a joke. In his current events class Bob explains how Africans looted and killed Asians in their Dar neighborhoods, and his students laugh. When Bob explains that the rioters are uneducated hooligans, the schoolboys sober up.

***

We've discovered a destructive pest. In the closet Bob finds a pair of his best slacks spotted with mold. I find mold across my one white tablecloth. Both pairs of our dress shoes are now white with fur as if they're sleeved in thin fuzzy socks.

***

In my kitchen there are no shelves for implements and spices. There's a desk-sized wooden worktable and a modest steel drain board beside the sink. All cooking equipment, dishes, dry goods and vegetables stay in the pantry and carting them back and forth is a big part of any food preparation. On the kitchen side of the pantry door, we have an upended packing-trunk-sized food safe—a wooden frame with two shelves enclosed in screen to keep flies or spiders away from bits of butter, cheese or leftovers that can wait till the next meal. By the time I grind meat or pressure-cook a stew and prepare simple vegetables, it takes at least an hour to make supper.

***

On January 30th a plane lands with letters from home and Mbeya food, butter, and fresh cream. For weeks we've had to use canned margarine that tastes like petrol and leaves a greasy film in my mouth.

The butter arrives just as I finish baking bread, so Bob's supper mainly consists of bread and butter.

*　*　*

Itch, itch, sniffle, sniffle—achoo! Bob's down with a cold, and I've got some sort of allergy. For the past three days I've had a bright red rash on my face, blood blisters around my mouth and puffy eyes that make me look like I've been crying for hours. I've tried calamine lotion and antihistamine tablets—to no avail.

FEBRUARY 1964

Mr. Mistry, our Indian science teacher from Gujarat whose wife speaks no English, pops by and invites us to Sunday lunch. We walk about a quarter of a mile along the tall grass-edged dirt path over to their somewhat older house that mirrors our own pale yellow cinderblock bungalow. Their two children giggle at the door when I hand them each a balloon. The five-year-old daughter skips about barefoot in a light cotton dress and the two-year-old boy pads along in a pullover shirt, his bare bottom diaperless. The family is Hindu, everything is vegetarian, and the meal must have taken all morning to prepare. We four adults sit at the dining room table, each of us facing a wide circular metal tray, a little water glass and a teaspoon.

Mrs. Mistry places a metal cup of thin yellow soup on each tray and gives us a flatbread *paratha*. The soup has a yogurt base seasoned with fresh ginger, green chilis, turmeric, cumin and garlic. A layer of sweetened lentils fills the *paratha*. We break off a flatbread segment, dip it in melted ghee and follow the sweet bite with a spoonful of tangy soup. Next, our hostess serves potato and onion *bhajias* (fritters) with coconut chutney. A lentil stew beside a mound of rice and spicy cooked cabbage fills the center of our trays. We gather balls of rice with our fingers and scoop the lentils and cabbage into our mouths. As I float on a carpet of enjoyment, I look across the table and see beads of sweat rolling down Bob's cheeks. Thankful there's no dessert, I couldn't have swallowed another morsel. I chew a cardamom pod from a tray of digestive whole spices.

***

We've arranged to ship the car—the crumpled Zelda—out on a large truck. It will leave February 3rd and will hopefully reach Dar on the 8th.

***

Bob is off for six days to an English seminar in Lindi over three hundred miles east of us. He left a couple of days ago in a Peramiho mission Land Rover along with five other teachers from surrounding schools. The group allows two travel days each way, since they may meet bad roads and the main bridge has been under repair. I'm lonely at home; it's the first time I've stayed here by myself. Insomnia is a frequent visitor, and for the past two nights I've dozed only an hour or two before morning. There's no electricity, so I can't get up and read. I've tried using a flashlight, but I spend all my time chasing bugs. Last night I took a Darvon, but it didn't faze me. I have one sleeping pill left from the burn incident and I'll try it tonight.

***

This morning I observe Mrs. Mistry cook lunch. She uses plenty of milk in sweets and yogurt. She gives me a small jar of yogurt for a starter culture, and as soon as I can buy fresh milk, I'll be thrilled to make yogurt following her instructions.

***

Saturday I get a lift into town after my class. I amble through the market, where vendors arrange mini-pyramids of tomatoes, potatoes and onions on crude wooden tables. I'm lucky to find someone with a gunnysack of limes. I look for a little cabbage or a few straggly beans.

I walk up the steps to Pardhan's shop for a spool of thread, then stroll over to Jen's. I sit down at her sewing machine and stitch on a dress I've pattern-cut from local cloth. This Singer runs by turning the main wheel with a hand crank as I guide the material with my left hand. I go over to Jane's for lunch and then return to my sewing for most of the afternoon. Later Jane and I walk to Maisie's for tea, until Noel drives me home, and the ho-hum life of small town anywhere takes up the hours of another day.

In town for a Sunday evening English service at the little church, there are only four of us in the congregation—three from the school and an Indian shopkeeper from town. We sit on low benches in the dim adobe chapel where a brass cross shines on the altar. A barefoot African priest reads Evening Prayer in halting English. Afterwards I put together a supper of pancakes and cheese blintzes for our four bachelor neighbors.

Monday we expect the Peramiho Land Rover back, and my casserole of Boston baked beans waits as I pace the floor in my new handmade dress. It's not till Tuesday afternoon that the Rover pulls in about five. Bob returns with a bag of oranges and coconuts. He tells me how excited he was to hear the lexicographer, A.S. Hornby, speak to the seminar. I tell him our galoshes have finally arrived.

* * *

It's mid-February and we're sweltering. This morning we attempt our usual Sunday hike, but after forty minutes in the hills beyond the school we give up. The dirt trails are dusty, and the air is heavy with humidity. We've had no rain for a week; maize stalks and beans in neighboring *shambas* look parched, wilting in the heat. We trudge back home in the quiet under the noonday sun.

***

This afternoon I discover a new blanket sealed in a plastic bag infested with moths. Tiny bugs get into all our dried foods. We've learned to put a bay leaf or a stick of wrapped spearmint gum in our tins of flour, rice or oatmeal to ward off weevils. We brush flies off our clothes as we dash into the house. I find the big bite on my left arm has become infected, so I've returned to the hospital for yet another shot of penicillin. Allergies still redden my eyes, despite drops the doctor gave me.

***

On Valentine's Day we throw a tea party. I bake heart-shaped sugar cookies and frost them with pink icing. Bob helps me make divinity candy, which we top with coconut and candied cherries. We're coming up to three Moslem holidays so there'll be no school Saturday or Monday.

***

Mrs. Mistry pays me a visit. I teach her how to make brownies and cinnamon rolls. She has never used yeast, vanilla or powdered sugar. She's surprised to see my gas stove and to watch me stand up while I'm cooking. I wish I had magazine photos of American kitchens to show her.

***

Rifle fire rattles the mornings while we walk to school. The army has established its third battalion in Songea. Their target-practice field sits next to our school grounds, and the racket pesters us. The influx of the troops brings a bustling *pombe* (beer) and brothel business to town. Villagers line up alongside the road near the camp to watch. We've been told the army is here to protect the border from Portuguese invasion. The Tanganyikan army supports freedom fighters trying to overthrow the Portuguese colonial regime in Mozambique.

On the radio we hear that American planes from the Congo have bombed two villages and a school in Uganda. Our government supposedly knew nothing about the disaster, and the planes may have been under Congolese control. However, the headlines published throughout East Africa declare, "American planes bomb Ugandan villages." More bad news: scandalous rumors are circulating about the deportation of two American consulate staff members from Dar. Add to this the fact that Washington has called home our ambassador.

Americans are labeled imperialist aggressors while Tanganyikan officials accuse our diplomats of subversive plots. No details have emerged, though we wonder how this could be possible. President Nyerere is currently on a state visit to China. Daily news reports bristle with his praise for the People's Republic. He's been quoted as favoring Peking's proposal for the reorganization of the U.N. When Nyerere visited the U.S. he saw industrial development far beyond what seemed possible for Tanganyika, but in China he sees factories with dirt floors and primitive equipment; this scenario seems realistic. To many Westerners, Tanganyika may be an obscure outpost, despite Nyerere's being one of the most influential leaders in Africa. If Nyerere aligns with the Chinese Communists, other African leaders will follow. In a local newspaper we pore over an anti-American editorial raging at President Johnson's lack of concern for Africa.

* * *

We join a group visit to Peramiho after I hear they have a surplus of lard. I'm lucky to buy two pounds for thirty-five cents. Plus, a Brother working in the butcher shop sells me a freshly made two-pound German *wurst,* a huge treat.

***

We invite two of my French students for supper this evening. They have an hour between their 6:15 roll call and 7:30 study session. We serve them beef stew topped with baking powder biscuits, then vanilla pudding with cookies. The menu sounds starchy, but we have no fresh vegetables except carrots and cucumbers these days. As Bob fills the plates and I lift my fork, one of the boys asks, "Will you please excuse me, madam, to use my spoon?" Abdullah starts to eat his bread and butter with a knife and fork, so we show them how we eat bread with our fingers. They down big portions of stew, and when he tastes our coconut orange cookies, Zuberi exclaims, "Madam, please, this is a wonder!"

Abdullah is from Mtwara near Lindi; his father tends a *shamba* where he grows rice and does all his work by hand. Zuberi lives in Masasi, inland from Lindi; his farmer father grows peanuts and cashews. They both ask if any farmers in the U.S. cultivate by hand. They also want to know if there are young Americans who've never been to school. They tell us that nowadays only government secondary schools are free; students still must pay to go to primary school.

They ask how many Americans know how to read, and tell us their village elders refuse to believe that the Earth is round. As they rise to leave, Abdullah gives an eloquent speech of thanks: "Sir and Madam, I am very grateful for this experience, which has taken me to another world. My classmates will surely not recognize me after I have tasted such tender meat with bread rolls on top." Zuberi chimes in with, "Madam, I am honored to have eaten American food that has coconut in a small cake." We hand them each a stick of Spearmint gum to tuck in their pockets as they head off to study for a history exam.

March 1964

Have you ever seen a real dragon? Today as we're driving home from town with Pillay, we see a giant chameleon inching across the road. Bright green and yellow, it stretches eighteen inches long and stands five inches high. Determined to bring it to the school, Rich and Vic coax the lizard to climb on a branch and stow it in Pillay's trunk. They claim the schoolboys will study the chameleon, but basically they want the beast as a weird pet.

***

Sunday evening the World Circle Club performs a series of original skits describing the workings of the United Nations. Our students memorize paragraphs from a UN booklet and dress up as members from different nations. Their costumes have nothing to do with specific countries but are a mélange of red plaid women's slacks, a white shirt, a green polka-dot tie, gray vest and a 1940's double-breasted tuxedo jacket, all straight from U.S. church rummage. After their skits the boys entertain the school crowd, dancing and singing their own made-up songs. We give them a raucous standing ovation for their rhythmic rendition of a tune about the ever-popular Canadian-produced East African brand name, Bata Shoes: "We can't make Bata. We can't make shoes. We can't make Bata Shoes."

***

Following an abrupt, unexpected transfer, the Mistrys pack up for another school in northern Tanganyika. We offer to buy their leftover food, but they insist on giving us rice, lentils, whole-wheat flour and a wealth of spices. With their two young children and clothing crammed in their tiny car, they have to leave a lot behind. Our clutch of teachers embraces the family as they leave their comfortable setting in a cloud of unsettled dust.

* * *

Sometimes I feel awful that Bob and I have so many comforts and most of the schoolboys here live without shoes, jackets and blankets. Aware that the headmaster has threatened to send home any boys who do not pay for their school uniforms, Abdullah asks us to loan him thirty-seven shillings. His only support comes from his Zanzibar policeman brother whom he hasn't heard from since the revolution. Bob hesitates to hand out money. I know I must let him make these decisions, but perhaps I can convince him to let the boys pay us back with native objects such as baskets or carvings.

A publication from the Afro-American Institute in New York has reached the school announcing funds available, based on personal letters from needy students. Dozens of schoolboys grab pens and jump on this project with supplications such as "My parents are the poorest parents in the whole wide world," and "I am an orphan, the poorest orphan in the world, and I am sure of it."

* * *

Tonight our Indian teacher friend, Pillay, stops by for pizza. It's exotic and new for him, as he insists I allow him to help roll the dough and scatter on the toppings. He works with the deft hands of a seasoned Indian cook. A few days later he invites us over for dal soup and curried chicken. I arrive while he's still in the kitchen and get a first-hand view of how to pop the mustard seeds and slowly brown the onions to finish the soup adding tamarind and coriander leaves. Now that's exotic.

Pillay's Dal

>
7 oz. (1 cup) Toor or Chana Dal or other
    Indian yellow or pink lentils

1 whole green chili

2 whole peeled garlic cloves

1 teaspoon turmeric

4 tablespoons vegetable oil

½ teaspoon brown mustard seeds

¼ teaspoon cumin seeds

⅛ teaspoon ajwain seeds (optional)

6 oz. (1 medium) onion peeled, quartered and thinly
    sliced (1½ cups)

1 oz. (large walnut-sized piece) dry tamarind (or
    rounded teaspoon concentrate)

1 cup diced fresh or canned tomato

salt, cayenne (chili powder), lime juice to taste

yogurt and coriander (cilantro) leaves for garnish

1. Rinse lentils and place in deep pot or pressure cooker with 1-quart cool water, green chili, garlic and turmeric. Pressure-cook or simmer covered until mushy tender. (Soak lentils in water for 1 hour to hasten cooking time.)

2. Heat oil in medium frying pan and sizzle mustard, cumin and optional ajwain seeds until they begin to make a popping sound. Add sliced onion and fry gently until onion is reduced and golden brown. (This will take at least 15 minutes.)

3. Crumble tamarind into a bowl and soften in ½ cup boiling water. When tamarind has cooled enough to handle, rub the fruit with your fingertips to form a puree. Strain the puree to remove seeds and skins. (Or use rounded teaspoon prepared tamarind concentrate.)

4. When the dal has softened. Add tamarind, chopped tomato, and salt to taste. Remove the chili and for added spiciness, chop the cooked chili and return it to the soup. Add 2 cups additional water if lentils seem too thick. Simmer 5 minutes.

5. Add seed scented oil with fried onion. Taste for seasonings, adding a generous squeeze of lime juice for added tartness, and a pinch cayenne or powdered chili for zest.

6. Serve the soup in bowls with a spoonful of yogurt and sprinkle chopped cilantro over the top. Serves 4-6.

***

We're mired in car insurance hassles. Apparently, the insurance company is in cahoots with the garage. We also haven't figured out how we'll retrieve Zelda since Bob can't find a ride to Dar. If he has to go by plane, it'll take a hundred dollars out of our three hundred and twenty-five-dollar monthly salary.

***

On Sunday in the middle of the month we become proud possessors of an honest-to-goodness refrigerator. I can hardly believe I won't have to make four or five trips a day to other peoples' fridges. Pillay, who will leave soon, has sold us his.

This antique marvel is a kerosene-operated three-foot-square box with a tiny freezing compartment that gets cold enough to make one tray of ice cubes or ice cream. We shell out forty dollars and it runs on two dollars' worth of kerosene a month, but we need to splurge. The first night we make lemon Jell-O and the next day mayonnaise for a cold tuna salad. The only glitch: cockroaches have infested the fridge's door insulation, and we can't figure how to get rid of them. With my next bit of cream, I'll freeze some ice cream. It will have to be a skimpy and economical version.

***

Today Songeans are saying, "We love our President." Ever since the January mutiny in Dar, President Nyerere's TANU party has demanded loyalty demonstrations throughout the country. Primary school children, our schoolboys, the police force, a women's association and mobs of villagers all parade to the Regional Commissioner's house. The pompous commissioner harangues the crowd. A pot-bellied representative of the Freedom Movement for Portuguese Mozambique incites cheers while children march to the rhythm of fifes and drums and the villagers join the tumultuous rally.

***

We had some full cucumber vines we hoped would produce, but now the leaves are withered and yellow. The soil teems with bugs and I've never seen so many flies. We spray our bedroom every night for mosquitoes before we go to bed. These bugs may carry malaria, which most native Africans have little protection against. Every Sunday we take two small yellow tablets of chloroquine, a quinine-based malaria preventative.

I wonder what it will be like not to have fifteen or so different bites that itch all the time. We've noticed a new species of ant. It only comes out in the dark. After I dish up supper, I turn off the kitchen light. When I return I find any pot or spoon left on the worktable covered with these critters. They scatter when I turn on the light.

***

A new fruit is coming into season: the guava is either light yellow or pink and pear-shaped. It has an intensely sweet fragrance, but like the quince it is better if I cook it. Pineapples are slacking off now; we've sure enjoyed them.

***

The rain has slowed to a continuous drizzle with on-again off-again cloudbursts the last few days. It's getting dark earlier and we've put a wool blanket back on our bed. Like the turpentine-flavored, mangos no bigger than hens' eggs that for weeks dotted the nearby forest ground and have now disappeared, summer's peak has passed.

***

This morning I set off on foot toward town to cook with my Sikh friend, Mrs. Singh. I take the shortcut path for a mile and a half. Soon I shed my raincoat, although the grass is still wet from the night's shower. A white-gowned old man outside his hut greets me, "*Jambo, memsab,*" as I bow, and four round-bellied children step out to stare. Five- or six-year-old boys bathing in the river giggle with embarrassment as I pass. Younger tots sucking juice from oranges scamper ahead of me, all but blocking my way. When they race away, I fear I've frightened them till I peer down at a solid mat of tiny stinging ants crossing the trail.

Once I join the main Matagoro/Songea road, a schoolboy pedals by, then slows down and waves me aboard. I hop on his back fender, and the rest of the way is "smooth sailing," even as his bike bounces over the rugged dirt main road to town. In the market square by nine, I bargain and fill my basket with bananas, cucumbers and sweet potatoes. I join the line waiting at the meat stall where today's hacked up, dark red beef carcass hangs from a roof beam, and the bloody-aproned butcher with his giant curved *panga* (machete) whacks off the next hunk of "steak."

The Singhs live in a whitewashed square house with a flat roof near the market square. Alas, Mr. Singh, our local postmaster, and his family will return to the Punjab in a few months. Like the other Indian kitchens I've been in, the floor is the cooking space. Mrs. Singh brings a bucket of fresh water from the single tap behind the house, where her husband just washed his hair and stands on the back cement slab turbanless with a thin shock of black hair hanging to his knees.

Mrs. Singh's mounds of onions and garlic wait in low baskets while she digs fresh ginger from a damp patch of sand beside the house. She has no fridge, but keeps her jar of curd (yogurt) from morning to evening in a pan of cool water. Into her bowl-like grinding stone still dusted with crushed cinnamon, cloves and cardamom, she adds handfuls of sliced onions, garlic, ginger and chilis which she pounds to a coarse mash with a heavy mahogany pestle. She likes the steady heat of charcoal, and when she wants a slow simmer, she sets a few glowing coals on the cement floor, places a pot on the coals and puts more hot coals on the flat lid for oven-like heat. I'm captivated by the smell of her gingery braised potatoes and nutty, ghee-brushed graham chapatis. I wish I were staying to eat, but on his usual Saturday drive to the post office, Vic comes by to pick me up at noon, and I'm home in time to make Bob an Adolph's Tenderizer–softened steak sandwich for lunch.

Songea Secondary School classroom building

Mrs. Singh's Ginger Potatoes

4 tablespoons vegetable oil

8 oz. (2 cups) peeled, chopped onion

1 chopped green Serrano chili including
    seeds (2-3 teaspoons)*

4 large cloves chopped garlic

1½ oz. (¼ cup) peeled, sliced and chopped fresh ginger

1 teaspoon ground coriander seed

½ teaspoon ground cumin seed

¼ teaspoon cinnamon

grated fresh nutmeg

½ teaspoon turmeric

⅛ teaspoon cayenne chili powder, optional

1 pound potatoes, peeled and cut in ½-inch dice
    (2 generous cups)

1 cup chopped fresh or canned tomatoes, or
    ½ cup canned crushed tomatoes

½ cup water

8 oz. (2 cups) diced zucchini or eggplant
    (2 small squash or 1 small eggplant)

fresh coriander leaves (cilantro) for garnish

* Remove seeds from chili for milder seasoning.

1. Heat oil in medium wok or large saucepan. Gently sauté onion until softened and beginning to brown.

2. Combine chili, garlic and ginger in mortar with generous pinch of salt and grind to a paste. Or place in blender with 2-3 tablespoons water and whiz to a paste.

3. Add ginger paste to golden onion and sauté until ginger smells cooked. Add ground coriander, cumin, cinnamon, nutmeg, turmeric and cayenne and sauté a few minutes until all spices smell fragrant.

4. Add potatoes, tomato and water. Season with salt. Stir and simmer covered. Add eggplant along with potatoes or add zucchini when potatoes are almost tender.

5. Taste for seasonings. Add more water if needed to make a light sauce. Use a bit of lime or lemon juice to lift the flavor and serve with coriander leaves, and yogurt. Serves 4.

* * *

When Lucas asks for Good Friday off as he's ironing, we have a serious discussion about Christianity. I'm astounded at how clearly he recites details about Holy Week and Easter. He's awed by Bible stories about the crucifixion, earthquakes as well as Lazarus and Jesus rising from the grave. He asks me where I go to pray, and when I mention the UMCA (Anglican: Universities' Mission Central Africa) church, he asks, "Memsab, do you believe in the Pope?" I read him the Easter story from the Bible, and he remembers having heard it in Mass.

Bob and I have lumps in our throats when he asks for shillings to buy an Easter dress for his mother—after we've given him his full month's wages in advance. He tells us he's sent these wages to his future father-in-law for the bride price without saving any for his own needs.

Although Good Friday may not be a time for indulgences, I'm going to take out a small tin of crab I've stashed away and make a Newberg with real cream, sherry and homemade patty shells.

* * *

I feel lonesome as I sit at the breakfast table on Easter morning, but Bob reminds me not to miss old things so much that we fail the see the scene before us. We read the Easter story from *Matthew* and I play Easter Bunny taking cookies around to the neighbors. We drive into town with Bry and Gil to the mud-brick church, which overflows with Africans from an earlier service. Most women wear iridescent chartreuse and pink Western-style dresses. They stride out of church chanting hallelujahs, clapping, letting out warbling whoops while the men, marching like dignitaries, sport long trousers, white shirts and ties. When the Father motions for us to enter the church, we're only a group of twelve for the English service. Gil offers to play the pump organ, and we all sing, "Christ the Lord is Risen Today." Later, Rich drops by for tea; Bob plays basketball; we listen to *The Messiah* on Mike's tape recorder.

* * *

These holidays make me wonder about the place of Christianity in African culture. Roman Catholicism, established by German clergymen, dates from the time Tanganyika was under German administration late in the nineteenth century. Nowadays an estimated one-third of the population is Islamic, another third is Christian, while others follow Hinduism or native spiritual traditions. Christianity as we know it is a difficult concept for many Africans. The Church says a man should have only one wife, but since women provide food and bear children, more wives guarantee a man greater status. Even in Christian communities polygamy prevails. The notions of moderation, saving and preparing for the future, are out of synch in Africa. Why worry about tomorrow when pests and poverty consume every day?

There aren't enough Christian clergymen in East Africa's innumerable villages, often no more than outposts of mud hovels, to affect tribal daily life. On the contrary, as long as one member of a Moslem village possesses a Koran and knows basic prayers, he can perform weddings, funerals, and other rites of passage.

Here ties of brotherhood extend family-like to members of the tribe, while sometimes violent hatred of other tribes roils through generations. This custom conflicts with the Christian principle of accepting and forgiving, let alone loving one's neighbor. Roman Catholicism may be stronger in the bush where Africa's uneducated village folk are drawn by an allegiance to the pope or a priest even when they may not understand the concept of an abstract God.

* * *

We enjoy a different view out our living room window each time we sit at the table. Mornings, we watch the mist roll away. At midday the sun blazes, and butterflies flutter around our zinnias while nest-building swallows swoop in under the porch roof. Towards dusk the trees shimmer silver.

April 1964

I load the oven this afternoon since I always try to make the most of our expensive bottled gas. Along with the mid-week batch of bread, I've planned to make a cherry pie for Bob. At sixty cents a can, tinned cherries are an extravagance. I open a new box of cornstarch, a Japanese brand I've never used. I measure the usual two tablespoons of cornstarch to thicken the cherry juice. It boils but doesn't thicken. I use two more tablespoons and still it doesn't thicken. Soon I've used eight tablespoons of starch. Zoom! It cooks solid—and tastes awful.

I can't waste a precious can of cherries, so I boil the thickened mess trying to cook away the heavy starch flavor. I add orange juice to thin it; Next, I drop in a bit of almond flavor, along with some lemon juice. Pretty soon it's quite good. When I add a dot of food coloring, the gray canned cherries turn bright red. Hoping that coloring will add some appeal to our dull vegetables, I spark up my dun-colored sweet potatoes with touches of red and orange, and when I add a few drops of green to my pickles they're luminous. With the box of food colors in play everything is "over the top" but tastes great—especially in dim light! We invite Vic and Rich over to share the pie and refrigerator freezer tray ice cream.

In Songea I made ice cream based on Junket tablets, a common form of rennet, but rennet is no longer readily available in supermarkets. This recipe presents a similar ice cream in its use of minimal cream and only one egg; it's more like frozen custard and cornstarch replaces the Junket.

Freezer Tray Ice Cream

2 oz. (4½ tablespoons) sugar
1 teaspoon cornstarch
tiny pinch salt
8 fl. oz. (1 cup) whole milk
1 organic egg separated
4 fl. oz. (½ cup) heavy cream
1 teaspoon vanilla

1. Mix 4 level tablespoons sugar with cornstarch and salt in small saucepan. Gradually stir in milk and heat to a simmer, stirring occasionally.

2. Whisk egg yolk with ½ tablespoon sugar. Pour a little of the simmering milk mixture over the beaten egg yolk, blend thoroughly and pour back into the hot milk. Cook stirring constantly until a light custard forms and coats the back of a spoon. Remove from heat; cool to room temperature.

3. Pour custard into a rectangular freezer tray or into a 1-quart rectangular or round Pyrex dish, and place in freezer until begins to turn slushy with ice crystals around the edge. Remove from freezer and stir every 20 minutes.

4. When the mixture begins to freeze with ice crystals all the way through, whip the egg white and fold in. Twenty minutes later, whip cream with vanilla and fold into the freezing custard base.

5. Continue to freeze stirring every 20 minutes until the cream is solid. Cover and retain in freezer. Makes a generous pint of ice cream.

***

As we sit at lunch, a dwarf-like man on a bike pedals right up to our front window and calls in to ask if we need eggs. His bundle of four eggs, wrapped and suspended on the cross bar of his bike, is tied with so many strands of bark that it takes him a full five minutes to undo the parcel. Later, a boy knocks at our door with a paper bag wadded at the top and held together with tape. He has three eggs plus green beans, which I buy for about thirteen cents. Another boy comes by selling bananas in the morning and mangos in the afternoon.

***

Saturday morning I catch a ride to town for supplies in the school truck and buzz all afternoon to bake for the schoolboys. They gathered $2.30 for ingredients, and I turn out two sheet cakes, a hundred and twenty peanut butter cookies and a hundred pineapple cookies. When Bob and I attend their evening tea party, we see slices of my iced cake decorated neatly with coconut served upside down on wet plates!

***

Today we hear that ants have killed the school's flock of chickens. During the rainy season we've noticed streams of black ants, sometimes pen-point tiny, sometimes bean-sized, marching along the roads. Often they invade our garbage can, turning it into a black drum; the next day they're gone. African ants have been known to kill elephants by climbing into their trunks and biting them to death.

***

Tuesday night we invite two of Bob's best students for dinner. They enjoy chili soup and a whole loaf of fresh bread. A lemon meringue pie astonishes them; they tell us that thousands of lemons rot because their countrymen don't know how to use them.

Having grown up in communal enclaves, most of our students don't seem to resent each other if one outdoes another. They appear content with themselves the way they are. It doesn't bother the few students who decide to drop my French class; they know they simply don't have whatever-it-takes to learn French. They're not at all ashamed of things that American students might try to hide.

***

On the way back from a staff tea party, we stop by the main hall where students are having a "social evening." They've rigged up a band with a guitarist, two drummers and a boy banging sticks together. They're doing The Twist wildly with nary a girl present. They dance with each other and gyrate from partner to partner. In fact, we've never seen men and women dancing together, only men with men and women with women.

***

Bob goes off to pay our water bill, but the office is locked before its usual two-thirty closing. Nevertheless, as he nears the window, he pulls the bill with its twenty-five shilling fee out of his pocket. When he sees the window is closed, he puts the bill back in his pocket but in the process drops the money. About an hour later as we're waiting for a ride home, he pulls the bill out of his pocket with its missing shillings. It's no use, he says, going back to look for the money; someone surely will have taken it. He walks back to the office anyway.

I continue to wait next to the door of Heradia's shop as I leaf through the latest *Time* magazine. A smartly dressed African man in a starched yellow shirt and a straw boater hat approaches me saying,

"Oh, madam, I see you like to read," and out of his brown leather briefcase he offers me copies of *Awake* and *Watchtower* magazines. Bob returns with the shillings, which he found lying on the ground untouched. We wonder if it's a reflection of quiet honesty, sleepiness in a country town—or Jehovah's Witnesses!

***

Pillay has taken a leave from the school, so Lucas is now working for us full time. It's going to be hard to find enough to keep him busy; up till now we've had help for only half a day.

I simmer barbecued ground beef for lunch, and since Sloppy Joe sandwiches are easy to eat with the fingers, I ask Lucas if he'd like to join us. He says, "Oh, no *Memsab,* I cannot."

After I smile, "Lucas we would like to talk with you while we eat," he savors a good lunch. Later, Bob and Lucas collect wire from Bert's place for a chicken pen. Bob's working right alongside Lucas when a gaggle of little kids gathers to stare at them. Lucas says, "See, sir, they are looking very hard."

Bob asks, "What they are looking at?"

"Sir, the children are surprised to see a white man digging with a shovel."

Bob replies, "Who do you think does the farm work in the U.S.?"

"Oh, Sir, You mean the white men even carry big sacks?"

***

Lucas can't find a home for his future wife. His father forbids him to build a house in his stepmother's village where he now lives. The father fears Lucas will give more money to his stepmother than to him. Lucas can't build in his father's village, since it's twenty-seven miles away—too far from school. He can build only where his own tribal ties will grant him land. He now hopes to find someone in a village near the school who will rent him a small house. He also needs to find tillable land, since his wife's job will be to cultivate and prepare food for the family. His wife will not be allowed to develop a *shamba* near a rented house unless Lucas buys the land, the cost of which would be prohibitive. We wonder if the wife might use some of the land behind our house, but we don't know if the school will allow it.

***

I stop by Matagoro Mission to buy eggs for Bob's birthday cake. I'm fortunate to purchase half-a-dozen, and, while making my way through the courtyard, I notice a giant tree laden with ripening fruit. I offer fourteen cents for six huge avocados to enliven our green salads and fruit cocktails. The avocado season will last for five months.

***

All our friends leaving at the term's end are packed and ready for the Wednesday plane, but in African fashion, not one has received a ticket let alone authorization from the ministry giving the headmaster permission to write warrants for their flights. They've sent numerous telegrams, have received no reply and there are only two days left. *Bado kidogo* (soon, in a little while)!

At last we say good-bye to four friends. We may get one replacement teacher sometime in June. The school will resort to having older students teach the younger ones for a while. Obviously seven teachers can't give adequate instruction to nearly three hundred students. Not only will the school suffer; we'll miss the company. Our friends in town, Jen and Arn left a month ago; Jane and Al will depart in July, and there's no hope of their being replaced by other Brits. Maisy and Noel, plus Bob and I will be the only young white couples in the village. One thing is sure: I'll be teaching, teaching, teaching.

Speaking of which: I received my first paycheck yesterday. For two months' work, my check totaled twenty-eight dollars—about seventy cents an hour. We hope there's some mistake; we can't even pay Lucas from my salary.

* * *

The term ends, and four of us crammed in Vic's VW bug make the two-day journey to Dar—Zelda's ready to roll again. My hair hangs rag-limp in the muggy air. I hand washed our underwear, and it's still damp two days later. We see our first movie in over a year. *Lawrence of Arabia* intensifies our view of this ancient Arab-settled African city. We envision robed men and women, camel caravans, and flute music issuing from incense-filled smoky shops—as tales of Arabian nights fill our imagination for days.

Unnerved as we are by the city traffic, we can't stop guzzling fresh milk and stopping for ice cream. We breakfast at the Luther House hostel where we stay, then lunch on bread and fruit. We buy five tangerines for seven cents. We've dined for two nights at a quaint bistro where cold lobster with homemade mayonnaise costs $1.50.

Three of us go for lunch to an Indian vegetarian restaurant, a clean, well-lighted place. We sit at an oilcloth-covered table where a white-tunic-clad server brings lentils, eggplant and flat breads for forty-nine cents a person.

On our earlier visit to Dar, I'd learned about *chapatis* only a few weeks previously. I thought how good it would be to try them again. I walked into an Indian restaurant and asked for *chapatis* and curd. The waiter shook his turbaned head and waved me off. I now realize that would be like coming to an American lunch counter and asking for crackers and ketchup.

106

***

Back on our own wheels, we travel north for the second try to visit Jim and Shirl from Grand Junction. Jim and Bob start talking cameras and before we know it, we acquire a Honeywell Pentax from a guy who sells cameras at huge discounts. Exhausted from wheeling and dealing with him, we now have a piece of equipment complete with light meter, telephoto and zoom lenses.

We stay an extra day as Shirl cooks an Indonesian meal of *Nasi Goreng.* We reminisce about Grand Junction High School when we hear their youngest child shriek from stomach pain, and we find him digging through my suitcase. The boy had opened a bottle of Dorbane that I had packed for constipation. He had chewed several of the bitter tablets and Shirl was quick with her nursing skills to encourage enough vomiting to empty his stomach—before we all turn in for the night.

Jim and Shirl are posted in Lushoto. High in the hills, the town looks like a German village tucked away by its green self. See-to-the-bottom brooks brighten the slopes as the smell of eucalyptus fills the air.

They don't agree with how the missionary school is run. When supplies arrive, Lutheran missionaries go through everything to ferret out what they want for their families. Apparently, boxes of clothing intended for the schoolboys remain stacked away in missionaries' houses. Most missionaries at Lushoto employ two full-time servants in houses more extravagant than the other teachers.

***

A six-hour drive over good roads to Mombasa brings us to the southern coastal tip of Kenya. In the city white-stucco residences with wood-shuttered windows and wrought-iron balconies hug the streets.

Corner mosques shade veiled women who glide past in black robes. Ever since the revolution, Zanzibar is no longer safe for a return visit, so we decide to hunt for Arab treasure here in Mombasa. We tread through a vast bazaar that swarms with gowned and fezed men. As a lone woman I walk with my eyes downcast. We barter and settle on an antique brass-studded teak money chest with secret compartments that's small enough for us to ship home. We empty our pockets for a prize reminiscent of Aladdin's lamp.

***

From Mombasa we follow the coast north to Gedi, the site of a thirteenth century Arab city, now a crumbling ruin. A hollow stone circle marks a drywell, and weeds grow over nearby foundation rocks.

The rain keeps us from most of the ruins as well as the beach. As luck would have it, on the rough road to Gedi, we knock a hole in Zelda's muffler and set out for Malindi where Bob finds a used muffler for three dollars.

***

After an easy slog to Arusha, we meet up with Jude, another TEAer from Grand Junction. How could it be that this program recruited teachers from all over the U.S. and chose five of us from small town Grand Junction, Colorado? Jude and her husband Hol tell of the bad-boy discipline problems they face in Arusha. They regale us with the story of their honeymoon through South Africa— until we know we have to get there, too.

May 1964

Twelve road hours later in Iringa we have the car greased. I do some food shopping and discover a bunch of wilted celery starting to turn brown. I can't resist the possibility of celery crunch and buy it to add to a can of bean sprouts I found in Dar for a chow mein. On my birthday we navigate the rutted Njombe Road over the Lukumburu escarpment toward Songea. We hit a rock, the new—used—muffler gets whacked, and we roar over the last few miles.

***

Official reports inform us of Tanganyika's new name. On the 26th of last month, Zanzibar united with Tanganyika forming the Republic of Tanzania. Shaky since the January uprising against the sultan, Zanzibar turned to the mainland and heads of both states forged this constitutional union.

***

When Bob comes home from town this morning, he tells me the African Father at the UMCA church has been informed that he'll be run out of town if he continues to conduct services in English for our small group. We ask no questions but feel a wisp of threat in the air.

***

Vic offers Lucas the position of being an inside-only houseboy. Lucas has helped us with gardening as well as housework, but it's a lot classier to work inside. We're sorry, in fact shocked, that Lucas is leaving. We've offered his job to Joseph, who's been unemployed since Bert left. I wish we had enough work to hire Joseph full-time; he's in his thirties and has a family. His excellent English will spoil us. He'll work four-hour mornings, and we'll see how it goes.

***

We invite the postmaster Singhs for Sunday dinner, their first experience with all-American food. I prepare fried chicken, mashed potatoes and gravy, glazed carrots, tossed salad, Parker House rolls and coconut pie. Our table setting with knives and forks presents problems for them, but they enjoy the meal—or so they tell us in hesitant singsong English. Decked in a black turban, Mr. Singh does most of the talking while Mrs. Singh sits primly in her flowing apricot sari.

***

I'm concerned about Joseph getting more work. I ask Jane if she'd like help, since her last houseboy recently quit. She now has Joseph in the afternoons, so he has a full day's work.

Joseph asks me if I have an old pullover or something with long sleeves that he might wear on these cool mornings. I look through our box of giveaway clothes and come up with a blue cardigan. I mend holes in the elbows and also find T-shirts for his children.

***

School starts tomorrow, and the term should race by with both of us on staff. I'll be adding two eighty-minute English classes each school day, and I'll have sixty essays to grade each week.

It's tough for my students to accept me as a teacher. Slowly they take "madam's" words as seriously as "sir's." Their names tell their religion. In one row I have Matthew, Peter and Paul; in another Hassan, Zuberi, and Mohamad. Sometimes old men from the village sit on the ground listening outside. They may not understand English, but they're lured by the tone of the session. Occasionally some of the school's cows pass poking their heads in the glassless classroom windows.

As I stand at the head of the class each day in my sneakers, socks, wool skirt, and sweater, I look down to see that only a few of the boys have shoes, much less pullovers. The desks and chairs are wobbly; the books are ragged. Most boys use twig and quill pens for writing. Much of the black is worn off our chalkboard, and a white dusty cloth serves as an eraser. I lean against a rickety table as the wind howls. When rain pounds on the metal roof, we can scarcely hear one another.

* * *

One day the boys sidetrack me, asking questions about life in America. There's no time for me to answer fully, so I suggest they each write out a question that we'll discuss later. As it turns out, I can't openly discuss such questions as "Why do Europeans wait to have babies until after they have been married maybe for several years?" or "What happens to all the babies the prostitutes must produce in the U.S.?" (Here it is common for a young woman to have a child before marriage to prove her fertility—and prostitution is everywhere.)

* * *

When shrimp and cream arrive on the Mbeya plane, we feast. We give ourselves a mid-week treat of French-fried shrimp and strawberry shortcake. The bedraggled canned strawberries are gray, but they taste OK.

* * *

There's an informal market on Sunday mornings after mass behind the Matagoro Mission church about a mile from the school toward town. Vendors squat on the ground with piles of bananas, trays of eggs and overgrown zucchini-sized cassava tubers. I've been looking for winnowing baskets, and this market is reputed to be the spot. We arrange to meet Lucas in the mission courtyard this morning.

It's Pentecost Sunday. I plant myself outside the doors and listen to the high-pitched chanting that makes me sway from side to side. With the relay of voices back and forth between the priest and the parishioners, I can't tell if it is Latin or Swahili. As soon as the service ends, the churchyard turns into a trading post. People wear everything from smart Western suits to ragged cloth wrapped around the middle. Young boys ply the crowd selling balls of greasy fried dough from wooden boxes. I bargain and choose two winnowing baskets and a hand of bananas. These wide shallow baskets of woven reeds rubbed red with clay, used for drying corn or winnowing rice, are a yard in diameter and four inches deep. They cost twenty-eight cents each.

* * *

This morning marks the first school *baraza* (assembly) of the term. The headmaster announces: "And now, boys, I am happy to tell you that we have toilet paper provided for all the latrines, so I don't want to hear of any more boys using maize cobs and leaves. I shall expect the prefects and the older boys to teach the younger boys how to use the latrines properly." The dormitories compete for tidiness awards, and the prize for the best-kept house is a mirror.

***

It's mid-May, the beginning of winter. Mornings, I wear my heavy coat to class, and I put on wool socks before bed at night. Bob has an awful cold. The usual remedies aren't helping and he's not eating well. He'll be stronger if he puts on a few pounds. It's so cold in the house the bread dough won't rise. Yesterday I put my bowl of dough out in the car, since it's closed up in the sun and warm inside.

***

I read a story to one of my classes about an African girl rescued from a poisonous snake. The students listen as if they understand, but when I question them the only answer I get is, "I didn't understand what happened." Later, I read another class a simplified Grimms' Fairy Tales version of Cinderella. This time my class is certain the stepsisters become blind because of their cruelty to Cinderella.

I don't have as much patience in the classroom as I hoped. Bob appreciates the pace of teaching here, but I keep wanting the boys to learn faster. As I've mentioned, our classes are eighty minutes long, and some younger schoolboys can't sit still that long. The other day I was red-faced when a boy stood at his desk and announced, "Madam, may I go out to urinate?"

Perhaps discipline problems in one of my classes come from my being the only woman teacher here. Women are the backbone of African life but do not command the same respect as men. Some older students don't think I have the right to ask them to be quiet. You should see their jaws drop when I tell them women are university professors and doctors in the U.S. I've had to resort to turning in a few names to the headmaster for a talking to.

JUNE 1964

We're expecting bigwigs from the ministry to be here Monday and Tuesday. Sutton and Peg, two of the visitors, are friends who invited us to dinner in Dar, and I want to return the favor. I'll do most of my preparations on Sunday. This afternoon I unravel a string of Swahili asking one of the school gardeners for my two pounds of peas on Monday instead of Saturday. He answers, "Righty-o *Memsab.*"

Sutton, a Brit, started out as a news reporter. He taught history and was headmaster for a few African secondary schools before becoming Tanganyika's Ministry of Education Inspector for History Instruction. He's the first person we met when we arrived and he told us we'd been assigned to "Post Fourteen." He plays the violin, speaks French and strikes us as a Renaissance man. Peg, his long-time companion, heads the Domestic Science Ministry. After teaching for decades in convent schools, she never lived in Tanganyika like Katherine Hepburn in *The African Queen.*

Sutton and Peg have vacationed in Provence, so I bust it to make a meal as typically French as I can. For an appetizer I serve "poor man's caviar," a mixture of baked eggplant mashed with lemon juice and olive oil. Of course French Onion is the soup. I make light dinner rolls and braise an Mbeya chicken for Chicken Niçoise.

Chicken Niçoise

1 3½ pound frying chicken cut into 8 serving pieces (make stock with back, neck, gizzard, heart.)

3 tablespoons olive oil

2 cups chopped onion (1 large onion)

1 tablespoons finely chopped garlic (3-4 cloves)

1 medium seeded and diced red or yellow sweet pepper

½ teaspoon fennel seed (crushed in mortar)

2 teaspoons chopped fresh thyme
  (or ½ teaspoons dry)

2 teaspoons chopped fresh oregano
  (or ½ teaspoons dry)

2 teaspoons chopped fresh tarragon
  (or ½ teaspoons dry)(optional)

pinch crushed red chili pepper

freshly ground black pepper

2 strips fresh orange peel, colored part only about 3 inches long (use a swivel blade potato peeler)

1 bay leaf

½ cup white wine (optional)

1 ½ cups chopped peeled fresh or canned tomatoes (14 ½ oz. can plum tomatoes)

½-1 cup chicken stock or water

salt to taste

pinch of sugar.

Optional additions: ¼ cup halved black olives, ½ pound sliced mushrooms, sautéed

1. Season chicken pieces with 1 ½ teaspoons salt and set aside overnight in fridge or 30 minutes at room temperature. Pat chicken dry with paper towel.

2. Heat 1 tablespoon oil in heavy frying pan and brown chicken evenly on both sides. Remove chicken to a plate and pour out oil.

3. Add 2 tablespoons fresh olive oil to skillet, add chopped onion, cover with butter wrappers and sweat gently until onion is translucent.

4. Add sweet pepper, garlic, fennel, thyme, oregano, tarragon, chili, pepper and sauté a few more minutes. Add orange peel, bay leaves, wine, tomatoes, stock or water, salt, sugar. Bring to a boil, cover and simmer for 30 minutes in the frying pan or in a heavy enameled cast iron casserole.

5. Add browned chicken pieces plus any juices, cover and simmer on the stove top or in a 325° oven.

6. After 30 minutes test the chicken breasts for doneness. If they feel firm and register at least 140° on an instant read thermometer, remove the breast pieces and simmer the rest of the chicken in the sauce another 20-30 minutes.

7. When ready to serve, return breast pieces, add optional olives and mushrooms, and simmer until hot. Check for seasonings, adding a little fresh lemon juice and more salt if needed.

8. Serve with boiled potatoes, buttered noodles or rice. Makes 4 generous servings.

We finish with freshly roasted African coffee. For a brief afternoon, we leave the confines of Songea and hike the rugged mountains in the south of France with Sutton.

***

The last time we were away the school gardener chopped down four trees near our front yard. Now dry enough for firewood, they offer kindling for nearby villagers. Right now two women are outside hacking the branches with their machete-like knives called *pangas.* They stack yard-long branches and tie the bundles with bark or twine. These women help one another heft the load of at least fifty pounds of wood onto their heads and stride off to their home fires, as I remember trying to walk across a room with a book on my head to help me learn better posture.

* * *

We plan to drive out to Peramiho this evening to hear the mission school orchestra perform Haydn's *Toy Symphony.*

* * *

Wednesday is my favorite day of the week. I have only one class in the morning. Then I warm the tub with hot water before refilling it for a weekly bath. We have a small bottled gas water heater that we light with a match each time we use it. It quickly heats only what water is needed, so there's no energy used in keeping water hot for later use.

* * *

We don't hesitate to leave Joseph alone in the house with our valuables or even loose change lying about. He's never taken a morsel of bread unless I've offered it to him. He's an excellent shopper and I give him a list with enough money the night before he cycles through town in the morning. He brings back no sales receipts but draws up an account of every penny spent and returns the exact change. He can often make purchases for better prices than I get.

Joseph is short and slender with a full head of hair, good teeth and twinkley eyes. He begins the day with a smile on his face as he arrives in his blue cotton shirt with rolled-up sleeves and lightweight navy cotton trousers. He wears black tie shoes but no socks and his slender fingers are quick with all matters of kitchen chopping, washing and ironing. He's been trained in British type household skills for almost twenty years, and with his fluent English, we enjoy storytelling as we work together.

This morning Joseph says he's unhappy working for Jane. He says the *memsab* is "cheeky" and "*karli*." He has decided to tell her he needs to fix up his house and can't work for her any longer. Jane will be here only for another month, and we tell Joseph he should stick it out and save the shillings for a rainy day. But he says, "I have three shirts, two trousers; my childrens have *chakula* (food) and clothes, so why should I work if I am not happy there? I will not tell her why I am leaving, but I will just laugh if she asks why and then she will never know." He says he'll be satisfied working half a day for us and that his pay, two dollars a week, is enough for his family of four. His wife is there to work the *shamba*.

He brings in the kerosene iron he bought from a moving sale. It's easier to use than our old charcoal iron, as he buzzes through a stack of laundry. I hand wash my school "uniform": red plaid wool pleated skirt and cardigan, and Joseph presses in the pleats this morning. We're trying to give him more work; we don't want to lose him to a full-time offer. Bob contends we should wash the evening dishes and sweep the floor ourselves.

* * *

It's hard to believe we've been in Africa almost a whole year. I'm not unhappy, but I can't help missing home. I don't realize how American I am till I find myself in a foreign country.

I think of my family sitting not far from the Book Cliffs in the summer sun of Colorado's western slope while we're shivering in the southern highlands on the other side of the globe. It's cooler at the school than it is in town, since we're on a hill and get more wind. I've been the laughing stock of the staff wearing wool slacks under my dress to keep my legs warm. I feel sorry for the students when I stand bundled in a warm coat and they're shivering in their shorts. Some schoolboys wear old tuxedo jackets with black satin collars, or they gussy up in women's suit coats fitted about the middle and puffed in the upper sleeve.

***

We've had typhoid booster shots. Bob's fine, but I've felt sick all weekend. I manage to keep my date to teach Mrs. Singh how to make fudge and divinity. Indians love sweets, but I can't teach her how to bake a cake since she doesn't have an oven. She's glad to stir a batch of slowly cooked chocolate fudge and to whip egg whites while I pour in boiling sugar syrup. When the white mass turns into a stiff cloud, we blob mounds of soft divinity candies onto waxed paper.

***

Mike, a new teacher, arrives. He's in his twenties, British, tall, with wavy red hair. He'll take over geography and has enticed us all with the prospect of a record player he's packed in his freight. He's out for a good time after the university drudge; no doubt he and Gil will soon be up to tomfoolery in the village. We now have three white guys with red hair on the faculty. All the staff houses are full, so Mike's in with Vic now that Rich has gone.

***

I've had my English class write some limericks. Here's one we worked on together:

> There once was a young man from Dar
> Who somehow got locked in his car
> Till a girl found the key
> That unlocked him when she
> Started singing about Zanzibar.

I've also taught a couple of classes the spiritual, "Swing Low, Sweet Chariot," which the students love to sing.

***

I'm alone this Sunday, since Bob and most of the other teachers have gone to Kigonsera, a school about 60 miles southwest of here. They're drawing up an exam both schools will take next month. I have papers to grade and tomatoes to can. We're having a bumper crop from the plants in front of the house.

***

A Polish family, the Oplustils, have lived in the village for twenty-two years. They own a sawmill and a flourmill where locals grind corn. They also sell building materials and animal feed. I invite them to our house for an East European dinner of borscht, Viennese goulash, rye bread, and a chocolate torte. We listen while they tell us their story in limited English:

At the beginning of the Second World War Mr. and Mrs. Oplustil were abducted from Cracow and sent to a Siberian gulag for two years. After they were deported to Iran, a humanitarian group brought them to a refugee's camp in Njombe, where they lived three years. In the bush of British Colonial Africa they spoke no English or Swahili.

They had to begin a new life in the wilderness. Mr. Oplustil heard that the Ngoni-Matengo Co-operative, Ngomat, was organizing in Songea. With his wooden leg, it took him three weeks to walk from Njombe to Songea. His wife soon joined him, and they eventually opened a sawmill. They added the flourmill four years ago.

The Oplustils have two grown children, twenty-one year old Kazik and Christine at nineteen. Christine has secretarial training from a school in Kenya, and Kazik has sights set on an engineering career. The Oplustils built their mills from the mud bricks up. For years the family's had one of the strongest businesses in this region, where grinding corn and millet is vital and where progress has created the demand for lumber. They've invested everything in their mills, but they haven't been able to find reliable workers ever since independence three years ago. They see the government taking over most of the industry in Tanzania. Songea has been their home for two decades, but as nationalization threatens Europeans they feel they must sell their mills and move to Canada before they become refugees again.

* * *

The school generator that gives us electricity four hours each evening breaks down. We putter around with candles and light a hurricane lamp that casts a smoky, yellowish light, straining our eyes; the smell gives us headaches. Lamp shadows quiver on the ceiling and walls in the ink-black night. We've never experienced such darkness void of any street lamp or nightlight. The schoolboys have only one pressure lamp in each classroom for homework. In the limited light they scrunch their desks together, huddling forward arm to arm, straining to read in a small circle. We've tinkered with candlelight and the hurricane lamp for days, and we're now told it will be at least two more weeks before the generator is fixed.

Following all the eyestrain and the nauseous smell of kerosene, we decide to see what we can find in town. After haggling with merchants in two Asian *dukas* for the best price, we settle on a German-made pressure lamp. Our new lamp has a cleaner kerosene burn than the hurricane, and we light it with methylated spirit. We pump the lamp every now and then to maintain brightness. It gives excellent light up to three hundred watts, as bright as a Coleman lamp.

***

We've decided to do a bit of day tripping rather than be such stay-at-homes on the weekends. We shimmy over rutted jeep roads, and I hold my breath as we ease over wobbly bamboo bridges. We head for Mlale, an Irish-backed settlement camp, which takes us one and one-half hours, thirty miles west. Like so many supposed grassroots plans, the purpose of this new community is to resettle Africans from crowded areas onto fertile land and to teach more productive farming techniques. As great as the idea sounds, from the way two Irishmen working on the project talk, we wonder if the scheme will fall through after the three years scheduled for its development. These guys say they spend their days trudging from field to field trying to encourage Africans to get on with cultivating their plots.

On the way back we stop at Peramiho where Bob picks up a pair of desert boots custom-made at the mission shoe shop. When I ask the procurator if he can spare a few things from the garden, he offers me fifteen pounds of oranges, a giant cabbage, a kilo of carrots and a few leeks— all for sixty-five cents. This vast walled garden has its bean rows in order and nary a weed in sight as I survey the bounty of produce that will feed multitudes.

July 1964

July 7, the Saba Saba (the seventh day of the seventh month in Swahili) marks the tenth birthday of TANU, Tanganyika African National Union, the only government-sanctioned political party. Friday and Saturday nights the school dormitories will present skits. Sunday, Monday and Tuesday will be school holidays with football games, native dances, speeches, a parade and a beauty contest. The celebrations are beginning early, and there have been tympani-like drumbeats in the air for days.

We drive into town for the Tuesday parade. The lineup includes primary school children, our schoolboys, and crowds of villagers. The primary children wear bright blue uniforms with hats and follow a drum major. The parade ends up at the Saba Saba grounds, a fenced open field, where everyone awaits his pompous highness, the Regional Commissioner. The police present arms; the ragged TANU youth group drills with wooden stick guns, and after a long wait, the RC drives up in his green, black and yellow Mercedes.

The RC is a giant balloon of a man. He's decked out in a beaded fur hat and flowing smocks. He begins his speech at noon. It's in Swahili, so we dash home for lunch. Back on the grounds in a jiff, we find ten tribes have set up areas for dancing, each with a flag on a stick, a smoking fire and a set of drums. It's always important to keep a fire going during drumming. The cowhide drumheads loosen with use, losing their tone. They tighten again when held over smoldering coals.

It's hard for us to imagine doing the same steps for hours or even days at a time. Girls shuffle in a circle as they take turns running back and forth across the ring, singing all the time. Another group with thick ankle bracelets of rattling seedpods as large as fist-sized kidney beans walks clockwise, then stomps and shakes.

The Matengo drummers produce such rich, deep-throated rhythms I can't resist joining their circle. There's only a smattering of dancers when I step in, but soon there's a crowd. The Matengo or Wadendeule drums are about six feet long, hollowed out from trees. The player first lays the long drum on its side and places his feet on either side of the drum top. He loops a heavy rope underneath the drum and around his hips as he lifts the drum, keeping the base open for a wealth of decibels. The drumhead hangs just above the drummer's knees while he leans forward to pound the hide-stretched top. His dancers stomp and sway as they shuffle back and forth, then side to side with knees bent and arms flapping to the beat.

Surrounding the Saba Saba field's edges, some reed and thatch booths display agricultural exhibits while others sell dried fish, sugar cane, fried dough or bread rolls and bars of soap or tins of milk. In the agriculture exhibits we see peanuts the size of cashews, basketball cabbages and the first big potatoes I've seen in Africa. I ask about the grower and luck out when I purchase a few pounds.

On the sidelines boisterous locals sell *pombe* (native beer) from *debes* (four-gallon square tin cans), pots and gourds. Everywhere people mingle in droves with their drinking baskets full. After they're first soaked in water, these tightly woven pumpkin-sized wicker bowls hold *pombe*. The beer, brewed from fermented millet, is the color of wet cement, as thick as a milkshake, and smells revoltingly sour. Someone holds out his basket and offers us a sip. Bob is brave enough to try, but I can't get past the smell. With *pombe* all around, the crowd is as tipsy as gang of dizzy teens.

Women flaunt frocks made from special Saba Saba cloth. One elderly gent wears a faded woman's housedress. When such a large group gathers, the deformed, the lame, the mentally handicapped come along, too. It hurts to see a young boy with a hydrocephalic head and such thin crippled legs he's only able to crawl.

We're the odd ones in this wild crowd, but we feel no fear as we make our way smack into the middle of the spectacle.

***

For months now I've been healthy, but I wake up this morning with a sore throat. Bob takes me to the hospital. The African doctor shoots me up with penicillin. He hands me a bag of codeine tablets and tells me to take two three times a day. When I had the infection in my foot last winter, one tablet was more than enough to knock me out for the night and most of the next morning. If I take six in one day, I'll be done in for a week. When I think of myself staggering in front of my class unable to finish a sentence, I think I'll just leave the codeine in the bag.

***

Thursday evening we invite Paul Mhaiki to dinner. He's just returned to Songea after a nine-month school year at Duquesne in Pittsburgh.

Bob extends the invitation to include Paul's wife, but since she speaks no English, Paul gives us the impression he'll come alone. Assuming she won't appear, I prepare for three. We're flabbergasted when she walks in the door with Paul. I add more broth to the soup, and we each have two meatballs instead of three.

We're interested in Paul's impressions of the States. He tells us he was accepted more warmly by white people in the U.S. than by Negroes. Many Negroes at Duquesne resented African students. American Negroes claimed that whites accepted Africans more readily than their own Negro countrymen. Paul eventually struck up friendships with a few Negroes, but he found it hard to feel close to them. He never adjusted to the helter-skelter of American life. He liked the food and sampled everything from hot dogs to pizza.

Bob and I listen to this man who grew up in a village of mud and thatch huts. Paul's command of English never falters as he twirls spaghetti onto his fork. His moon-faced, wife says little, but joins the conversation with smiles, nods and intermittent claps. She enjoys the dinner and has honored the occasion by wearing her traditional dress in green-and-purple patterned cloth and a matching bow-tied headscarf.

***

On a Sunday morning hike we stumble on four boys pounding tin cans alongside girls dancing outside a hut. They seem to be having fun, so I walk over and start dancing, too. Soon they're giggling, and I'm surrounded by at least twenty women who join in the singing and twisting to beat the band. More women rush up the hill from their shambas when they hear the singing. At first I worry that the women are going to stare at me suspiciously, but soon they join in. They don't seem to mind my being here; one woman even tries to give me a shilling, but I return it to her. Everybody wants to shake my hand and they whoop like cheerleaders when we walk away.

***

Once again we're sitting by lamplight. The head gasket on the generator has blown for the second time. I hate to say it, but repairs tend to be shoddy when things get "fixed" here. With the head engineer gone, it may be eons before the generator's up and running again.

* * *

Bob calculates that our total living expenses for last month came to $100. That's less than we paid for a month's rent in California.

* * *

A recent *Time* magazine pictures the prime minister of newly independent Malawi, Dr. Hastings Kamuzu Banda, holding two objects of African regalia. In his left hand, you see a flywhisk, which he holds like a scepter. The whisk is made from the long hair segment of a zebra or cow's tail attached to a carved wooden handle. The whisk is meant to repel flies, but more often it stands as an emblem of authority. In his right hand he holds a decorated ebony walking stick. Poor folk may use a tree branch, while the wealthy and powerful use carved ebony or ivory for walking sticks.

* * *

Bob puts his interest in anthropology to a test when the regional information officer visits the school. He shows Bob a cloth bundle of human bones unearthed by prisoners on a digging project near a tree in the village. Stories start to surface about a mass grave.

When Germans seized control of Tanganyika and placed tribes in slave-like conditions on plantations decades ago, native groups joined in a mass uprising known as the *Maji-Maji* Rebellion (1905–1907). Through a series of mythical tales, the Africans believed they were immune to European bullets if they were sprinkled with sacred *maji* (water). Chief Songea led the Wagoni, a Bantu tribe that had migrated north to this area from Zululand during the ferocious reign of Chaka the Zulu in the nineteenth century.

At the height of the *Maji-Maji* Rebellion in our region, the Germans tried to appease Chief Songea with bribes after massive numbers of Wagoni were not able to fend off bullets with *maji*. Martyr-like, Songea declared he did not want to live under European rule after so many of his people had been killed. Accordingly, Songea and his five remaining chieftains were hanged, and one solitary tree was planted as a memorial on the site of the mass grave.

When bones are discovered sixty years later, village elders retell the event and let it be known that nothing should be disturbed. One old man recounts how eight days after the hanging, he and three others were given a cloth-lined box and sent out to return with Songea's head. Out of fear, rather than resisting the colonial Germans, he unearthed Songea's head, washed it in a nearby river, enclosed it in the box, which he nailed shut and presented to the *Boma* (regional government office). He assumed the box was shipped to Germany.

Today Bob and six of his schoolboys venture to the site. They unearth three perfectly preserved molars, plus a few bone fragments. Villagers stationed nearby shake their heads and grunt disapproval till the would-be anthropologists climb out of the pit. The schoolboys try to tell onlookers that they're helping preserve an historical site. Further excavation awaits permission from Dar, and there may be plans to dedicate a monument here to the Wagoni chiefs.

***

People keep telling us it's exceptionally cold this year. We now have five heavy blankets on our bed, one underneath us and four on top. Our feet are chilled all day, and it's hard to warm them at night.

***

We take a weekend outing to Kigonsera to have lunch with the Guptas, an Indian couple. Bob met them a few weeks ago when he traveled an hour and a half west for an exam meeting. We've sent them a letter, so they're expecting us.

Mrs. Gupta has prepared lunch with her curry powder made from fennel seed, cinnamon, cardamom and cloves. If it sounds strange to use pastry spices for meats and poultry, they're absolutely delicious. The Guptas don't have a car and may not be able to come to Songea in return, so I've filled a box of home-made sweets for them, including a Mexican orange candy, fudge and coconut ice. Again we realize how much more we have than most people on the planet. The Guptas don't have enough forks or cups to go around for the four of us at their table.

***

Our houseboy, Joseph, tells us his wife has disappeared. Christian churches stress that a man should have only one wife, but an African, Christian or not, often takes two wives to be sure that if one runs off there will be another standing by. Here in the bush divorce is non-existent, so husbands and wives separate and remarry at will. From the way Joseph tells it, adultery is as common as prostitution. Joseph's young children are staying with his brother's wife for the day while he awaits his wife's return.

***

It's ridiculous that I packed three pairs of tennis shoes and five pairs of high heels when I left for Africa. The tennis shoes are holey, and the high heels are covered with mold. Whenever I put on a pair of heels, I limp. My feet aren't used to fashion anymore. I've learned to wear sandals and go barefoot in the house in summer, though I don't want to chance meeting stinging ants outside.

***

Thursday afternoon: A blue Mercedes pulls up next door, and two friendly guys ask for a place to bunk overnight to avoid the local hotel, The Angony Arms (known by the locals as The Agony Arms). A few curious teachers gather to meet the strangers. Tom, an Irishman down from Nairobi who sells drugs for Roche Ltd., is on safari to supply government hospitals in the Ruvuma region. Ren has come along for the ride. He's French and teaches African history at the University of Florida. Tom regales us with easy- going chat, as Ren chimes in with theories about tribal life. The group ambles over to our place for tea, and new English speaking faces light up a humdrum afternoon. We hear how two freewheeling young men jaunt through the bush towns of these southern highlands, going for days without seeing white faces, learning to eat local food and sleep on mats in small hospitals. They're both starved for talk.

***

I don't know what to think about the Republican convention nominating Goldwater. His isolationist ideas aren't realistic. Maybe we can't "legislate morality," but a civil rights bill is something we must put forward, as I realize more clearly than ever here in Africa. Bob and I ponder the campaigns but won't be able to vote this year; we haven't written for ballots early enough. One thing is sure: my hat's in the ring for LBJ.

***

This morning a pamphlet from the Ministry of Education has been distributed to all our classes. Chock-full of long sentences, the English language leaflet is intended to awaken the schoolboys to Tanzania's "national endeavor." Apparently, students should pay attention to five concepts: Competence, Moral Character, Putting Knowledge to Useful Purposes, Imagination and Fellow Feeling. The five-paragraph pamphlet takes forty minutes to read since the boys have to look up every other word in the dictionary. In my second class I ask the boys if they've read the pamphlet. They tell me their teacher read it to them. I ask if they understand it. They don't have the foggiest notion about what it means.

***

This afternoon we lunch with our Sikh friends, the Singhs. I ride to town with the school truck to observe the preparations, and Bob comes by around noon. The Singhs from north India are so different from our western Indian Gujarati friends, the Mistrys. When we dined with the Mistrys, we ate with our fingers from large stainless steel trays set with small bowls of condiments. The Singhs use plates and two spoons. A large soupspoon serves for a spicy chicken and rice dish with curd (yogurt). We eat the second dish of curried potatoes and unleavened flat breads (*chapatis*) with our fingers. We tear the *chapatis* into pieces and use them to wrap around chunks of saucy potatoes. The small teaspoon serves for an almond vermicelli milk pudding dessert.

At the end of our meal, Mrs. Singh tells me she'll give me her pestle, *chapati* board and rolling pin when the family leaves for India next month.

***

Bob constructed a small chicken run after we bought three Rhode Island Red hens from Mrs. Oplustil. It's all but impossible to purchase eggs during the rainy season. Local eggs stored for days in the heat spoil and their shells break easily because village hens often have a poor diet, scratching about for insects and seeds. Our well-fed hens get out for grass and bugs each morning, and we collect one or two large eggs every day.

In Dar I bought a preparation called "water glass," a sodium silicate compound that dissolves in water. If I submerge eggs in the liquid, they'll keep for weeks. We'll ask Joseph to gather the eggs and add them to the water glass bucket while we're away.

***

I've just cooked up a Mexican dinner for Hare and June, the AFSers who think they're going to be transferred to Dar. Preparing Mexican food over here is a bit of a stretch. Chili powder's available everywhere, but the Indian and African version of chili powder means powdered cayenne peppers. It's HOT and must be used in pinches rather than spoonfuls. Yet a little of this powdered cayenne mixed with paprika, cinnamon, cumin and oregano makes a pleasant blend—another lesson learned.

***

We hear that one of our teachers, a Brit, is hospitalized at Peramiho for infectious hepatitis. He'll have to stay there in isolation for three weeks. Maisie says that either hepatitis surfaces as a serious individual infection or an epidemic of light cases. Now we're all wondering if one of us will be next. I feel fatigued and a bit flu-ish, but I don't have any yellow creeping over my skin, so I guess I'm OK for now.

***

I feel another sore throat coming on. We drive to the village hospital for penicillin, and the doctor tells me to stay away from school for three days. That's too long; we have only two days before exams.

At times like this I'm thankful for Joseph. I haven't said anything to him, but when we come home from the hospital he has little meatballs in tomato sauce simmering for lunch. He returns toward evening to fry a steak for Bob and boil an egg for me. In fact he now says *chakula tayari* (food is ready)—it's time to eat.

***

Joseph may be underpaid, but by local standards he earns more than his neighbors. He owns a bicycle, a transistor radio, plus a house with a *shamba.* He has shoes and shirts while his neighbors wrap themselves in cloth and go barefoot. He knows if he's short of money we'll give him an advance. He had a sniffle yesterday, so when he didn't show up this morning, I assumed he stayed home with a cold. When I returned from afternoon classes, he was standing by the sink with his hands in dishwater. He said he knew he had work to do and it was not good to lie in bed all day.

Bob and I disagree about whether to pay Joseph while we're away. Bob may be more thrifty than I, but we must at least keep up a subsistence wage for him if we hope for his loyalty, and it will be good to have someone keep an eye on things while we're gone.

***

Joseph burst in this morning exclaiming, "Oh *Memsab,* do you know what I've been hearing many people say in the town?"

Witchcraft is brewing in the bush; we'd heard it first from Pillay. Now the townspeople as well as schoolboys are dazed. Two weeks after Mhaiki's return to Songea, Acting Headmaster Mbenna, greedy for power, decided to turn to black magic. The story is that Mbenna and one of the African teachers brought a black rooster to a *mganga* (witch doctor) late one night. The ritual took place near Matagoro

Mountain, high on a granite cliff where deformed newly born babies were once left for the gods. Hidden in darkness, the *mganga* killed, bled and stewed the rooster into a potion with herbs and roots. Mbenna drank the broth and fell into a trance under incantations and the sorcerer's ceremonial feathers, blood and beads. The *mganga* put a hex on Paul Mhaiki. He would either die, fall seriously ill, or be transferred to another school. Mbenna would again become headmaster.

Some say the story leaked after a TANU youth leader heard a rumor and, hidden, observed the ceremony. Others say the friend accompanying Mbenna feared for his own life when he heard the death oath pronounced and told the authorities. The black magic took place about a month ago, and the witch doctor is now in prison. The Regional Commissioner pressed charges, and the witch doctor eventually confessed. The education officer has gone to Dar to resolve the problem, and no one knows what will happen. We feel concern for Mhaiki; he must be terribly frightened. Mhaiki and Mbenna, both Catholics, have counseled with one of the mission priests to make a settlement, but in East Africa talking does not abolish fear. The battle lines remain. A hex is a hex.

We talked to one of Bob's students yesterday and asked if he thought the scandal posed any real worry. He said the power of the witchdoctor is definitely still alive. Witchcraft, he told us, became unlawful only three years ago, and legal decisions do not change ancient culture. While the British were in charge, they thought this concept of sorcery was sheer hooey. But after independence African leaders, steeped in superstition and afraid of their power-hungry countrymen, continued to use wizardry to usurp one another. The abuse of negative magic pushed the government to make laws condemning witchcraft.

* * *

Today Paul Mhaiki officially takes over as headmaster again. He wants to live with his family in his own house a mile or so from the school. The Ministry of Education, however, has ordered him to move onto the school compound, so he'll have more of a show of authority and they'll collect more rent. It's clear that in the wake of the witch doctor scandal, Mhaiki's presence needs to be evident round the clock.

***

As Massudi writes in an essay about fear: *"Nearly every tribe believes in supernatural forces. This is widespread in my village and Tanganyika as a whole. When a person begins a journey and meets a one-eyed person for the first time, the traveler postpones until the next day. This means than any one-eyed person always brings unhappiness or bad luck to the traveler. For the same reason some people say that a traveler is likely to be unfortunate if he meets three people at the same time, or one person without a load, stick or anything in his hands. But two people at a time prove that the traveler will be successful.*

Most elderly people are afraid of white people. This is true with women nowadays as most men seem to have been accustomed to seeing European commissioners, etc. Some people are also afraid of Indians who are today the most regarded traders. Europeans are feared because almost all people believe that white people are in search of a country to rule.

The greatest fear which is not being well understood and a little unknown to some others is rockets. Most people become very scared when they see a rocket for they believe it to be a war starter. They say that each rocket has no man in it, but is filled with war instruments such as loaded revolvers and atomic bombs such that when it reaches a certain place, it will fall down and kill many people."

***

135

Massudi continues with a long discourse on the traditional method of making pottery, which *"generally takes about a week, during which time the potter and the person who will own the pots is not allowed to do several things: Both are not permitted to sleep in one bed with their husbands. This is most applicable to the buyer, for a pot maker can use certain kinds of magic to prevent any damages to the pots. The woman who will own the pots is not allowed to take part in adultery until the pots pass through all stages of preparation. Anyone who has mated with another is not allowed to visit the place where pots are being made. Nobody is allowed to urinate or to bury feces in the area where the pots are to be burned."*

***

Neither of us has anyone to talk to about personal problems. We feel distant, forgotten, and each day we try to be patient with one another. I feel as if I'm going down the drain. Bob tells me, "You're psychologically shot." The honeymoon of our adventure has passed, and we're into the long slog of our day-to-day routine. I'm ashamed of the cloud hovering above me. Sometimes I choke back tears, give myself a good talking to, and keep moving through the next hour as best I can. I manage to keep busy, but loneliness creeps up and homesickness pries at my backbone. I don't know why depression has come over me or why Bob has developed stomach troubles. He finds it hard to keep down food and to sleep. My only break from the humdrum is to cook, and now Bob has no interest in eating. Two weeks ago when the Irish Roche drug rep and his French buddy were at the school, I risked asking about Bob's problems. The rep suggested Libraxin to relax stomach spasms.

***

We usually pick up Voice Of America or the BBC, but today we tune in to Radio Peking. Chinese radio describes American aggression against the Democratic Republic of North Vietnam. The Chinese contend our criminal acts have been on the drawing board for a long time, and President Johnson is using gunboats to stay in office by gaining the support of Americans who want war. Peking urges all peace-loving peoples to unite against U.S. imperialists. The Chinese accuse Americans of supplying weapons to the Portuguese in Mozambique and causing trouble in the Congo. Radio Peking and the Voice Of America contradict each other. What are our African neighbors to believe? A few villagers own transistor radios, which they listen to by the hour. Although most don't understand English—the Chinese broadcast in English— there is usually someone to translate.

***

The Congo threatens African/U.S. relations. Massive demonstrations, encouraged in Dar and reported in the nationalist newspaper, *The Tanzania Standard,* give way to the headline "Yankee Meddling Is Turning the Congo into a Bowl of Blood." The paper carries photos of demonstrators' placards: "You Dirty Yankees, Stop Killing Our Brothers!" and "To Hell With Imperialism Headed By American Yankees!"

AUGUST 1964

Mao recently toured Africa. The last time we were in Dar, the city teemed with sprucely dressed Chinese in Mao jacket-like shirts. At a large Chinese industrial exhibition Nyerere accepted fifteen million pounds sterling worth of military aid from The People's Republic. Nyerere claims he is moving forward with the policy of African socialism and non-alignment. He asks Western countries to stop opposing him when he accepts Chinese aid and reminds them that Peking doesn't cry out when he accepts West German aircraft for his new air force. Tanzania is willing to accept aid from anyone who will give it.

***

The only vegetable we've found lately is green onion, and I'm lucky to buy a bundle of small potatoes for French fries Bob says are too good for ketchup.

***

We have a staff meeting tomorrow, but we're not sure when we'll be able to leave, since several African teachers haven't finished their marking. Bob gets peeved at their *bado kidogo* attitude. I wish he wouldn't tie himself in knots; we aren't in a position to change things. Sometimes I think he would make a good administrator. He loves to organize and keep things tidy.

* * *

It's August 12, our second wedding anniversary. We load up Zelda, make room for a passenger and head west over the Njombe Road. Back in December and April we slithered through mud on this road; now we jounce over washboard dirt tracks and use the windshield wipers to remove dust rather than water. The countryside is burnt umber as we pass grass fires in the bush. This controlled burning drives away wild animals scavenging food close to villages. We heard that a leopard prowling near the school a few days ago killed a village child and was later hunted down by Kazik Oplustil, son of the Polish miller.

* * *

From Njombe we veer northwest another hundred and thirty-five miles to Mbeya. One of our African teachers traveling with us invites us into his extended family's neat mud-brick house. He introduces us to his relatives and shows off his family *shamba* devoted to corn, onions, rice and papaya.

Although food and mail have reached us from Mbeya for almost a year, this is our first visit. We wander in and out of shops, open deep freezers and gape at Danish chickens, legs of lamb, sausages and ice cream.

* * *

The second day we zip two hundred and fifty miles north across an arid plain alongside loaf and pillar rocks mushrooming out of the landscape like phantom Stonehenges. Once in a while we see people perched on the crest of a tabletop stone. The desert town of Singida appears to be a forsaken clump of soot-stained wattle and daub hovels crumbling at the corners. There's scarce town traffic and shops appear shuttered. There's no hotel, but we've been told to stop at the

Lutheran mission where someone might offer us a spot to throw our sleeping bags. In fact, the director leads us to an empty house with space for the night, and an American family invites us to share supper.

I feel like an alien in this house where I see a bowl of artificial fruit on the table and a woman wearing American costume jewelry. The décor is straight out of *Better Homes and Gardens*. The living room has a sectional sofa, piano, Hammond organ and pole lamps. There's a generator on the compound; houses are wired with one hundred ten volts for American washing machines, mixers and Singers. We relax in cushioned luxury, and dine on tuna noodle casserole.

***

In the morning we blaze north across the grayest, flattest, most desolate space we've ever seen. Here and there in this landscape with no grass, trees or animals, we pass mud huts with plopped-on grass thatch roofs that look like scarecrow hats, as well as roadside walkers draped in dusty black cloth. This year has been especially hard when the rains stopped early and the people harvested only one crop of maize. Cold as we were in Songea, today the desert heat is stifling. We bump along for hours. We stop for stale water from our thermos and a roadside lunch of pork and beans from the can. Mirages float on the horizon. We're sure we see water, a palm tree, a cloud above waves of heat.

***

At Mwanza on the shore of Lake Victoria we strike up an acquaintance with a guy who offers us a bed in a Peace Corps hostel. We're tired and hope for an iota of quiet, but, wouldn't you know it, by one a.m. the rooms explode with volunteers who've come to the city for a weekend of partying.

Bleary in the morning, we leave the hung-over late sleepers and charge east to what we remember as our favorite spot in East Africa—Serengeti. This time we trundle in from the Mwanza side to visit areas we couldn't get to during the rains. In August the park is an arid adobe-hard plain blackened from fires. There's been no rain, and we find no herds of wildebeest, zebra or gazelle.

Early this year the government raised park tariffs, yet tourist masses have started to migrate here. Last November only six other campers joined us in the self-service lodge where we threw our sleeping bags on bare bunks in chilly concrete cubicles and walked down the path to communal showers and loos. Now a modern tent city has been set up. No longer a camping spot, Serengeti Park is well on its way to becoming a posh resort with air-conditioned rooms and typical English lodge food. We meander over roads on our own and zoom our lens on two cheetahs playing under a tree.

Leaving Serengeti is no cause for sorrow, we tell ourselves, as we climb into tropical rain forests around Ngorongoro Crater barely visible in cotton-thick fog. The narrow road reminds us to turn on our headlights and honk our horn while we snail's-pace forward, aware a lorry may whip around the next blind curve.

***

For weeks we've been planning to climb Mount Kilimanjaro. We decide against a top-dollar hotel-arranged tour. Following the advice of friends, we bring our own warm clothes, sleeping bags, and food. We rent boots and a Primus stove with pots and hire porters at the Kibo Hotel in Moshi. We leave the hotel by 9:15 in the morning and make our way up the first twelve steepest miles of the climb.

We pass Wachaga coffee *shambas*, where women carry loads in tightly woven baskets with leather-strap handles banded over their foreheads. As they lean forward, the weight rests on their upper backs. We trek through a forest and cross a moor. We reach the first hut by three in the afternoon, ready to stretch out and rest.

We share the evening with six climbers. At suppertime, I forgo the Primus and hunch over a smoky wood stove with an African cooking for the hotel group. After tomato soup from a packet and fried tinned corned beef on toast, we clean up and retire to men's and women's sections for an early lights out.

In the middle of the night something hits me. I rush out of the hut. Other women offer me medicine, but nothing seems to work. It's cold; the ground's a mud wash. It's been raining throughout the night. I need to get up and go outside more times than I can count. Soon I'm weak, unsteady, and when I need all fours to make it back up the steep steps to the hut, my boots slide and pull me into the mud. I try a wash-off in the icy stream, but I have no towel. We've brought one flashlight, which Bob has in the men's quarters, so I stumble in the dark, crazy with the continuing urge to squat.

Dawn arrives, but I'm too sick to care. We decide to hunker down. Late that morning when I feel better, we pack up and head out. A couple of hours later we pass the worst part of the climb for that day, but ten miles lie ahead of us, and I'm fading. I run behind the bushes every twenty minutes; my legs begin to quiver till I realize I can't go on. A shadow of sadness looms over both of us as we turn around. Bob keeps reminding me that I'm more important than Kilimanjaro. I feel like lying down, but I keep creeping and slowly, slowly we walk back to the hut where we spent the night.

One of our porters offers to return to the hotel to request a Land Rover for me. But we know that after this much rain even a four-wheel-drive vehicle could make it only halfway. We send the porter back anyhow and try to baby-step down the mountain. Our porter meets a Land Rover stuck like a godsend in the mud. If I can make my way to the driver, he'll take us on to the hotel. I crank up every bit of energy I can muster and inch down to the Rover.

Back in Moshi we return to the house of the TEAers where we stayed Monday night. They're not home but their houseboy lets us in. The way I feel, this is no time to be in a hotel. Bob rustles up sausages with eggs for his supper, and I try to force down some bread and milk. We each take warm baths, and I go to bed with Vaseline rubbed on my raw bottom and a hot water bottle on my tummy. Around midnight an attack hits Bob; he's doubled up vomiting, with violent stomach contractions.

The houseboy tells us there's no European doctor in Moshi. I phone the library, and an English lady directs us to an Asian doctor she says is reliable. We wait on a stone bench in the doctor's clinic crowded with *kanga*-wrapped African women and crying babies. When it's our turn to go in, I wonder if I'm in a doctor's office, a magician's chamber, or an alchemist's laboratory. The walls abound with shelves and tables lined with boxes, bottles and jars of all colors. There's no nurse, no sterilizing machine; only a small kerosene pressure stove flickers under a steaming pot. The doctor doesn't speak much English but we use sign language. He doesn't write out a prescription and send us to the pharmacy but picks up scraps of newspaper to wrap three white pills for Bob and three yellow ones for me. He dips a spoon into loaf-sized wooden boxes of powder and mixes up a dose of mystery medicine, then wraps everything in more newspaper. He tells Bob to swallow glucose tablets before trying any food and says I should eat only boiled rice and yogurt sprinkled with cumin seed for a day.

Boiled rice and cumin are easy enough to come by, but yogurt is something Indians make at home; it's not sold in any shop. When I ask an Asian boy working in a store that sells fresh milk, he says his grandma might help out.

We arrange to meet at the car park in front of her apartment house. Bowing before her, I accept a red bowl of yogurt and agree to return the empty dish to her grandson the next day. The rice with yogurt tastes good and seems to restore balance to my ravaged GI tract. The powders and pills do their job, and in a few days we're back on our feet. We're still not sure what hit us.

***

We need to be in Dar by Monday the twenty-fourth, so we convince ourselves we're well enough to make the trip on Sunday. It's a gut-jouncing drive from Moshi to Dar, but we make good time despite extra-rugged stretches of corrugated roads. By mid-afternoon we revel in a graveled section of new highway. We sail along like kids on a holiday till all at once I hear a thud and let out a cry. In one of those instants I know I'll recall for years, I realize I'm alive and open my eyes to find my dress sprinkled with glass as blood trickles down my forehead. Bob has miraculously guided Zelda to a stop at the cliff edge of a deep ravine, his eyes saved by sunglasses. As I shake his arm I scarcely remember the car speeding down the hill, toward us. One of its wheels must have tossed up a rock that hit our windshield, smashing it into countless shards like a broken bowl. We open the doors and step out to shake glass off our clothes. Unaware of what's happened, the driver who caused the accident has disappeared over the horizon.

Two cars pull up alongside us. A white woman my mother's age uses a handkerchief to wash my forehead. She fixes me up with Band-Aids while the men rag-wrap their knuckles and knock the rest of the glass from the corners of our windshield.

We're still one hundred twenty miles from Dar, and there's no garage man around the corner who could pop in a new glass. We have no choice but to bandana our heads, put on sunglasses, push on and pull over to the side of the road, shading our faces from dust whenever another car approaches.

We learn this type of accident is so common here that we must pay extra to get windshield coverage on our policy. We study our insurance and discover we've been driving for the past ten days on an expired policy. Bob renews the policy the next morning, adds the extra coverage and puts in our claim that very afternoon. Aside from scrapes, our fearlessness has perhaps been the biggest victim in this, our second car mishap within a year.

***

Four days in Dar pass like the aftermath of a bad dream as we shop for sandals, food and wine to lift our spirits. With a new windshield and our dignity restored, we embark on the journey home, this time south along the coast, then inland west to Songea.

We overnight in the port city of Lindi and push on to Mtwara to meet three American women at the girls' secondary school. These TEAers have such enviable tans that I stroll to the beach hoping a brief lie-down will give my skin a rich healthy glow. The sand is warm, the sun blankets me in brightness and a breeze through the palm trees lulls me to sleep at midday. After an hour I wake with a start, feeling as though I'm in an oven. All night I sweat and shiver, sleepless, swallowing aspirin.

***

The next day we pull up at Ndanda mission, a Benedictine Abbey with a school and hospital. A nun doctor in a black habit insists I soak my seared self in a tub of what feels like icy snow melt for half an hour.

By evening I'm coherent enough to chat with an elderly Sister who's been teaching at this mission for forty years. She tells me her Benedictine vows allow only one eight-week family visit outside the abbey in her entire life. Her face's wrinkles draw upwards toward her eyes as if she's beginning to smile.

Bob sleeps in the Father's priory while I luck out with a feather bed in the convent where we're served a cold supper of home-made sausage, potted meats, sauerkraut and pickles in the guests' dining room. The next morning we tour the mission schools and dabble in American slang with a buoyant young nun from Nebraska who directs the middle school.

***

Thankfully, with car and beach mishaps behind us, with two days on the road ahead, we're hoping to reach the American Salvatorian mission near Tunduru this evening. First, we plan to see one of Bob's students. He drew such a good map it looks like it leads us to his door.

About half a mile from Tunduru the road becomes little more than a goat path. We leave the car under a tree. Alongside the first mud hut on the right, we call out for Yusuf. He answers, whereupon we step over a threshold into a mud-walled brown box of a room where the short, shiny nosed Yusuf grins, "Hello."

After shaking our hands he continues to push a charcoal iron over his laundered trousers on a wooden table. He offers us stools and describes how he built this house by himself during the school holidays last December. It's customary for a teenage boy to move a short distance from his family's house and construct his own dwelling when he's fourteen or fifteen. He joins the family for meals but tends to all the rest of his needs in his own place. This practice gives more space for younger children in the main house.

He shows me his outdoor kitchen where a card-table-sized plank tops four bark-free branches planted on the ground. Clean upside-down plates and cups, an aluminum kettle and a couple of saucepans without handles sit on the table next to a bucket of water—the sink—on the ground.

We ask to photograph Yusuf with his mother and sister, but he says we must first meet his grandpa. The bush telephone system moves ahead of us. Children, ever-present, scurry over to their elders, and by the time we arrive at Grandpa's house, the veranda has been freshly swept and two chairs set out under a mango tree. Grandpa, clad in a tan safari jacket and a wraparound *kanga* skirt, presents us with a traditional small hen before we promenade as a foursome to the main house for photographs. We set our hopes on snapping shots of the grinning *totos* (children) in their everyday clothing. By the time we ask permission, the girls have changed into little cotton dresses with gathered skirts, puffed cap sleeves and sashes, and they're posed on the family porch.

* * *

Before dusk we pull into Nandembo Salvatorian Mission. Two American churchmen who visited our school a few months ago, welcome us like old buddies. Compared to Ndanda and Peramiho, Nandembo is a poor neighbor where supper is served at the unlikely hour of six instead of the usual seven-thirty. Bob says he's "starving"! The Salvatorians are based in Milwaukee, so it's an American mission house and we're at ease with French fried onion rings, meat loaf and banana cream pie.

Sleeping bags come out again for the night, and in the morning we walk around the Mission's dry fields and sparse vegetable garden with no flowers. The newly built mud-brick classroom building has fresh whitewash and a tin roof; inside, plank benches and tables suffice for desks. The young Brothers, Pete and Cole, stride about in bluejeans and plaid work shirts as they tell us how they built this school from its hand-shoveled foundation up. I spy three mulberry trees loaded with fruit by the bank of a stream and ask if I might pick some.

I know I'm surrounded by flies, but right now I don't care. I pull down mulberry tree branches and gorge on berries till my hands and mouth are black. Soon I've picked a bagful, which I place atop our luggage before we set off. At home, I find berry juice has trickled all over the sleeping bags and the back seat. I scrub stains from the upholstery and canvas sleeping bags but still have enough fruit to cook up two glasses of jelly for our morning flame-grilled toast—plus a mulberry pie.

September 1964

We return to Songea and find the countryside even more drought-stricken than when we left. Joseph has looked after our yard, but a layer of dust coats everything inside our house. Despite tiny black sugar ants that have invaded our pantry shelves, I'm ready to be off the road. In the evening grass flames and cooking fires fill the air outside with the smell of smoke.

**

I'm happy to have a new American family here: Joe, Marie and their two kids. Joe is stubby and round; Marie is tall and large-boned. She has little interest in food, and I can't believe she's happy with their houseboy's grim cooking.

Joe and Marie have been here only a few days before their two-year-old drinks a cup of kerosene. Marie sticks her finger down the girl's throat to make her vomit and rushes her to the town hospital to have her stomach pumped, but she's sick for days. Now both Marie and her infant are in Peramiho Hospital after the baby came down with dysentery. I can't imagine how he contracted this bug while still being breast-fed.

**

After Labor Day school doors open in America the same day as they do here. Winter is behind us; we shed our sweaters and wool socks.

During my first English class there's a knock on the door; it's the headmaster. He gives the boys a stern talking-to about not working hard enough. He summons laggard students to his office for "strokes," lashes for their laziness. I'm more shocked by this announcement than the boys.

* * *

I hear a rap on the front window. I look out at a man in a floppy straw hat, with a basket slung over one arm. His face is scarred with rickrack lines over his cheekbones and forehead. With a toothless smile, he asks, "You like to buy Makonde carvings, *Memsab*?" as he beckons me to come out and view his wares.

The Makonde people, the most renowned carvers in Tanzania, live between the southern highlands and northern Mozambique. I'm captivated by the round-headed, flat fertility dolls. Women who hope to become pregnant strap them to their bodies. Men hoping for protection from their mothers or wives in this matrilineal society wear them in their clothing. I strike a deal with our carver. He loads up his bag like an itinerant Santa, and I plant two dolls on our mantle.

* * *

The Oplustils invite us for dinner. Mr. Oplustil, with his reddish tan leathered face and grease-stained heavy twill work pants, listens to the news every hour and speaks at length about world affairs. He praises Goldwater and is rabidly anti-Communist after what he faced in Poland and Siberia. Mrs. O, round and aproned, in a flower-print cotton housedress and sensible shoes, greets us with warmth and the handshake of one who has weeded gardens and kneaded bread dough for decades. They keep a heavy hand over their nineteen-year-old daughter, Christine, while their son Kazik at twenty-two is wild-bird free.

Christine had told me earlier how she longs to be around people her age, but her parents want her to meet a Polish man. She knows they won't find him here, so she's waiting until the family moves to Toronto. She's devoted to her family, but I feel her gritting her teeth as she rises in tight jeans and T-shirt at her mother's request to refill the water jug. Kazik glows with a deep tan. He loves bushwhacking beyond jeep trails, and I can't help but wonder if he doesn't have a secret life in the village.

Kazik and his dad recently butchered a pig; we dine on breaded pork chops with cream gravy, rice-stuffed cabbage, potatoes, and a cold beet relish. The sweet/sour flavor of the relish plays out my portrait of this family stuck in a place that once offered hope but now estranges them.

***

We're enjoying Joe and Marie. Joe's knowledge about the German occupation of Tanganyika fills in our history gaps. Marie lets her two-year-old play in the dirt and track dust through the house. She sits with the baby and reads. Her nursing skills give her confidence she can manage illnesses common to this part of the world.

We plan a tea party for Tuesday afternoon so they can meet Maisie and Noel, who are expecting a third child. Everyone cheers when I produce a plate of glazed donuts, which the Brits claim are one of the best things to come out of America.

***

Songea's international enclave has a big Saturday night. To celebrate their twenty-seventh wedding anniversary and their daughter's twentieth birthday, the Oplustils throw a party for transplanted Europeans, Americans, a few Asians and Africans. I wear a black and white silk dress with high heels. Bob wants to put on his black suit, but we've forgotten to take it out of mothballs. For the first time we drive through town at night and find the darkness broken only by an occasional hurricane lamp flickering in a window. All's quiet on this southern front, except for guitars twanging at the village dance hall.

When we arrive at the Oplustil's cinderblock bungalow built on one side of their mill, twenty of us fill the main room cleared of furniture. Only a parson's table loaded with liquor bottles centers the room. Booze is the big thrill in these parts, but Bob and I each find a single gin and tonic enough. It's surreal to see everyone dressed up, away from our usual faded cotton housedresses and farmer-type duds. Gil's out in a full kilt with lacy cuffs on his shirt.

We're elbow to elbow, lifting drinks to toast our hosts till around nine-thirty when the liquor bottles push back to make room for platters of roast pork, cold chicken, and an array of Polish salads. We heap our plates and soon find the table refilled with almond cakes and rice pudding. The excitement keeps us going until the crowd drifts away after eleven-thirty. I'm glad I wrapped up a foil-covered box of fudge and macaroons as a thank-you package.

* * *

Bob is master on duty for evening roll call and dining hall inspection. I tag along to see what the schoolboys have for supper. At mealtimes every student brings his tin plate and bowl to the dining hall where cooks dip meat or bean stew into each bowl and heap each plate with rice or maize flour porridge. Tonight I notice the soup is as thick as gravy, and the schoolboys mix the soup into the rice, or they make balls of rice to dunk into their soup. Several boys offer me a taste. I dip my fingers into a few bowls and find the beans zipped with a bit of curry powder. The food here, some students tell us, is better than they get at home.

***

I'm giving my English classes speech practice with one-minute impromptu talks. It's tough for them to speak English without having written something beforehand. They're all willing to give it a try, not at all bashful about standing in front of the class. I assign simple subjects such as telling friends at home what they do in school or describing how a crop is planted.

As they talk about crops, they fumble to find English words for peeling, husking, and shelling. They don't know the English terms for cultivated places such as orchards or groves and fields or gardens. One schoolboy writes about the seasons: *Tanganyika as a whole has two distinct seasons. We have hot, wet summers from November to April and cool, dry winters from May to October. Most interesting is how uneducated natives can foretell the approach of a new season.*

During their dry season, they know when it ends although ignorant of the months of the year. There is a type of tree around the area which when the wet season approaches, sheds its leaves and so when the natives see these trees starting to shed their leaves they begin to prepare their farms or shambas for the rainy season. In some places this type of tree is very rare. Instead of trees they use birds to forecast the seasons. There is a bird of the "hornbill" type which nests during the approach of the rainy season.

***

My students ask me what a yam is. I describe a large orange sweet potato and compare it in flavor with the white sweet potato grown here. They laugh out loud. Sunday morning I greet one of my students,

152

Hamisi, standing at our door. He's holding something that looks like part of a log. He tells me the "log" is what he calls a yam. I thank him and hand him a couple of tomatoes in return. I'll ask Joseph about this yam tomorrow.

***

The next day Joseph appears at my classroom with anxiety written on his face. Bob and I glance down the hill to see flames leaping around our house. The grass fire is already too large to beat out with a gunnysack, and we know it will have to burn itself out, while people watch to keep it from spreading. I dash home and move the car. By noon roof-high flames dance in front of our living room window. After lunch the fire line has crept to the back near the chicken pen. Bob lights the patch of dry grass behind the house and lets it blaze, while we stand nearby. Nothing flammable remains within ten feet of our walls. Later that afternoon a carpet of black ash surrounds our cinderblock house with its tin roof.

***

One of our office clerks, Ubulini, has had three weeks to run off some French exercises for me. This morning at last he tells Bob they're ready. As loud and slovenly as Ubulini is, we've lent him money and have tried to be courteous to him. The only time he allots me to pick up my papers is during our eleven-o'clock tea break. I rush to the office to get the copies for my afternoon class. Ubulini is taking his tea break early. He's stuffing himself with fried dough cakes and gulping cup after cup of tea. I ask him if he might give me my copies; he claims he's terribly hungry and can't put down his cup for a minute. I wait for him to finish a couple of cups and ask again more firmly. No, he claims it's his break time and he can't help a busy lady. He doesn't care that I've had no tea break. I'm bursting to pick up the stuff, but he won't tell me where it is, and the office is such a junk heap I don't know where to look. I storm off.

Bob tries to collect the copies later, with no luck. We turn to the headmaster. Ubulini convinces him that I'm at fault. Ubulini would have had to wash his oily fingers before touching the papers and that would have taken more than a minute of his precious free time.

***

I've been saving a canned ham that my mom tucked in our sea freight. When some fresh cream arrives from Mbeya and I know I can make a special dessert, I invite Noel and Maisie to dinner. I take the ham out of the closet—we don't have any kitchen cupboards and since the pantry shelves are all open, I've kept the ham tucked behind blankets—and there in bold letters on the front of the can I read the words, **PERISHABLE. KEEP UNDER REFRIGERATION**. I turn the can over and read, "This ham will keep indefinitely unopened under refrigeration." Alas, it's been in the closet for a year. A ham is a treasure here. I open it. It doesn't smell bad. I sample some, which tastes briny, but not spoiled so I take a bigger bite. A day later I'm still ticking, without a tummy ache. I cook the ham and serve it for our dinner, though I guess I won't use it for Noel and Maisie—except a smidgeon in an appetizer.

October 1964

I find myself getting so aggravated with my students these days I dread going to class. It's just as hot for them as it is for me. During afternoons the boys are sleepy; they might accomplish as much if I let them put their heads down on their desks for a nap.

During fifth period after we read aloud and discuss a few paragraphs, I ask half-a-dozen people the same question before anyone can give me an answer. In French the boys refuse to do a stitch of work. Low grades on tests don't concern them; after all, their education is guaranteed once they're in secondary school. Much as I struggle against their complacency, I come home and try to cook off my frustrations, but Bob's lost his appetite.

***

Our chickens are laying like troupers. We get three eggs every day; right now I'm over a dozen ahead. I'd better savor them while they're here; this golden abundance won't last long.

***

The witch doctor case has resurfaced. A government lawyer arrives to hold high court proceedings in Songea. The accused, Mbenna, his co-conspirators—the East German–trained information officer and the witch doctor—hire a lawyer from Dar to defend them.

The trial takes place in the village UMCA (Anglican) church, the only room in town with benches, a podium for the magistrate, and seats for the accused. We observe the proceedings one afternoon. As we make out bits of Swahili confessions and tall tales, we realize the spectacle has turned into a social parade; village men wander in and out of the court room sporting cast-off western women's fancy dress coats and feathered hats. Mbenna and his cohorts are blasé and receive a slap-on-the-wrist fine of three hundred shillings. The law takes its course; the thick veil of custom overshadows change.

***

This morning something hits me in the gut. I wake early with such a painful stomachache I'm sure I've been poisoned. I'm in misery all day, but have no diarrhea, no vomiting, no fever. Marie brings over paregoric, which puts me to sleep. Later in the afternoon a visiting missionary lady doctor pokes around my stomach but finds nothing remarkable. I nibble the smallest morsel of toast with tea. By late afternoon I make myself a bit of custard. Too miserable to read, I swallow codeine to get myself through the night.

I'm better now, though still shaky. As I lie here, I remember when I was in sixth grade and had trench mouth. I was so sick my mom had to feed me by placing a cloth over my blistered lips. Without touching my lips she spooned in mashed potatoes, crushed pears and milkshake—all this despite her exhaustion as a night-shift RN at the VA hospital.

***

I buzz over to Maisie's to see if I can help with the christening party. I find her in a cluttered living room feeding the baby while two other kids squall. Her houseboy has suddenly taken sick, and she's on her own hosting a party for twenty. Luckily she's done most of the cooking, but she's been counting on Alius to bake bread and tidy up. I volunteer our Joseph for the day and return home to turn out three dozen Parker House rolls plus two braided loaves. After Joseph irons my black dress and shines our shoes, he cycles over to Maisie's. I remove Bob's black silk suit from its mothball bag, and Marie does up my hair in a French twist!

To arrive in good English time we don't leave home till after eight. Noel has set up a bar on the veranda where we all gather. At ten o'clock the dining room doors open and reveal a buffet table groaning with ham, chicken and salads. For dessert we sip glasses of bubbly along with sponge slices, fruit and cream. We settle over coffee, and someone suggests dancing. Our hosts own a record player, and we're soon twirling and twisting around the living room as midnight passes. Near one a.m. Maisie cuts a pink-and-white decorated christening cake shipped from London, and we savor slices of English fruitcake with marzipan. The guest of honor, wee as she is, hasn't been seen or heard since her party started. An hour later I gather up my bread pans, and we bid farewell.

***

A paperback book comes in the mail. For a couple of days I take an excursion with John Steinbeck. Four years ago Steinbeck outfitted a camper truck. With his dog, Charley, he set off to see as much of America as he could. He stayed away from big cities, national parks, tourist sights. He wrote about truck drivers and lonely waitresses at highway cafes. He found a wandering game warden and a house trailer mechanic. From Maine and "the New York Island," he drove to the Pacific. Returning through the South, he made his way back to the eastern seaboard. Here in East Africa I've devoured *Travels with Charley* like a chat with folks at home.

***

My French textbooks arrive at last. Every one of them is gorgeous! This is the very same text I used when I was a student teacher at Long Beach State. When I learned the books were not being used anymore, I wrote to the Long Beach Junior High French Club. They bought twenty books for a dollar and raised $15 for postage to ship them overseas to me.

First, I'm set on teaching the French national anthem in the book. The boys have never seen a sheet of music, and when I ask them about the little black figures lodged between the set of five horizontal lines, they haven't a clue. When I explain how music is notated, they're flabbergasted. They play native instruments; they sing and dance but they've never seen an orchestra, except in a movie. Even so, they don't believe musicians are "reading" music. They think musicians play from memory like the boys who play flutes and drums in the school band. I get carried away talking about music. I go on about the importance of art and spirituality—and they moan like bored teenagers.

For them science rules the world. They can't grasp social science or the notion of someone being "neurotic," much less "psychotic." They think insane people are morons who are born that way and are meant to be laughed at. The concept of someone strong in body and sick in mind is as alien to them as the concept of living room television.

***

I think I've finally mastered Hollandaise sauce. The trick, I've learned, is to use a heavy glass bowl atop simmering water rather than a standard metal double boiler. Metal heats too fast and the sauce scrambles.

***

We shared an apple today. We brought one home from our last safari. It's been hiding in the fridge for two months after it traveled all the way from Australia.

*　*　*

Late Sunday morning Bob packs the camera. I gather enough candy, bananas and balloons for four children, and we set off. Joseph meets us at the village bus station and directs us to his house about a mile away. We park Zelda by a little river, hoof it across a log bridge and up the hill to a cluster of mud houses. I don't want to call them "huts," because a number of them are quite spacious. Joseph's wife, kids, and neighbors have turned out to greet us. We feel like royalty shaking hands and *jamboing* everybody.

We enter a tidy sitting room where wooden chairs with red cushions await us. One wall holds two rows of family shoes hooked on nails: three pairs for Mama, three for Papa. A hot water bottle and a kitchen strainer decorate another wall. Farther back a full bookshelf meets our eyes, including a collection of four cookbooks. On top of the bookshelf a transistor radio sits like a crown jewel, along with a wind-up clock and an assortment of empty wine bottles and coffee jars. Some of this stuff must have made its way out of our trash box.

The kids stay outdoors; Mama sits shyly in a corner while Joseph shows off an album with photos former employers have taken of him and his family. In the album we also check out certificates of quality for the bicycle, radio, and even the hot water bottle.

He invites us to sit at a square table with a tablecloth, forks, spoons, teacups, sugar, milk—the works! I hoped he would serve us African food, but he says his wife disapproved. Instead he's stewed chicken with carrots, potatoes and tomato sauce. The chicken is tender or "soft," as he likes to say, and familiar vegetables swim in a soup. He adds a side bowl of boiled beets, then offers tea and bananas. The plates are chipped and the cups mismatched, but the three of us eat and drink together like old pals.

Bob clicks a special lens into his Pentax, and we go outside to capture the scene on film. When the children gather round, I hand out bananas, candy and balloons. I join Joseph's wife pounding cassava. We plant ourselves on either side of a knee-high wooden mortar and take turns swinging pole-like wooden pestles.

Joseph's half-brother lives next door and runs a small bakery. He's filled his mud oven with firewood, and when the wood burns to coals, he scrapes them out and places bread or cakes on the oven floor. The mud walls absorb enough heat to bake dozens of sizable bread loaves. Each morning the brother loads up a cart and pushes his wares to town where he sells bread and muffin-like cakes. After a walk around the neighborhood with Joseph and his wife, we cross the log bridge and wend our way home through parts of Songea we've never seen.

* * *

Every day after classes drums throb around the school compound as the boys prepare for their annual dance competition. During the blistering performance afternoon, they carry on full-tilt from three to six. Each of eight groups has to be forced to stop after twenty minutes. I've talked to schoolboys about dancing and have had my classes write compositions about their dances. I keep expecting to find "hidden meanings"—prayers for rain, fertility rites or magic. I don't find allusions such as I've found in American Indian dances. In this part of Africa people dance because they're happy, and that's all there is to it.

The Swahili word for dance is *ngoma,* which might translate literally as "a game for fun." The schoolboys find the concept of "dance" in English hard to grasp as a noun and a verb. They write, "We played a dance," when they mean to say, "We danced." Each tribe has its local *ngoma,* though the Twist remains the national favorite, just as it's the latest dance fad in America. Here in Songea even boys on stilts twist.

***

The new Parliament representative for Songea arrives with his exotic West Indian wife, who causes a flurry among the men and boys. Her skin is *café au lait,* and she parades about in a Tanganyikan national dress with a long tight skirt, a low-cut sleeveless bodice and a pleated peplum at the waist. I hear she speaks only French and minimal English, so I attempt a tête-à-tête with her. Alas, my French is so rudimentary that she chuckles. At one point I boldly invite her to our house. She replies, "Well, we might possibly think about it." I shut up after that.

***

This evening Bob's World Circle Club puts on two amusing skits about how laws are made and how important it is to pay taxes. In between the skits, schoolboys sing and show off their dance routines. My French class contributes "Frère Jacques."

***

At first the Ministry of Education refused to recognize my American degree and paid me one hundred dollars per month. Later they decided to accept the degree and gave me two hundred a month. Their most recent letter says they don't approve my degree and are reducing my salary to one hundred again—plus, they'll take back anything they paid me over a hundred a month. I must swallow my pride and devote myself to the cause. Right now I don't know what "the cause" is!

On payday my salary is not only diminished, but I'm not even summoned to the office. No, the headmaster calls Bob in and gives him MY check!

November 1964

After last week's dance fest, we're aching to buy a *Wadendeuli* drum carved from a large tree trunk. These prized drums will not be easy to purchase. We ask Nathan, a schoolboy, to come along to help negotiate in Swahili with the *wazee* (old men).

Twenty-five miles east on the Lindi Road we find a jiggling circle of dancers near a few huts. The *ngoma* has been gong on since yesterday afternoon; by nine this morning the space reeks of *pombe*, and the bleary dancers are bug-eyed. They make a to-do over us *wazungu* (foreign visitors); everyone gathers round to shake our hands. Women let out war whoops of welcome, and men come over to serenade me with rattles and hip wiggles. I hesitate to join the dancing this time since everyone's tipsy. Bob is more cordial and sips from *pombe* bowls. A woman with an ear-ringed toddler clinging to her *kanga* presents me with five tiny eggs. She holds up a copper-colored winnowing basket, which I offer to buy.

Some women dancing with babies slung over their backs are so drunk their *kangas* have slipped, leaving their breasts open to the breeze. When Bob takes out his camera, one woman puts on a show by rolling in the dust.

Three large drums pulse, but no one is interested in selling. One guy asks us to drive him closer to his house; he says he'll fetch something for us. We load him into the car, bid everyone farewell and proceed up the road a few miles. He gets out at his village and says if we return in a while, he'll have a drum for us. Our schoolboy, Nathan, warns us we'd better not depend on this fellow.

162

Farther up the road Nathan meets his father, who gives us directions to a house where an old man tells us he has two drums he'll consider selling. Nathan says they're bigger than what we want; he doesn't think we'll be able to fit them in the car. We start to drive away, but Bob decides they're worth a look. He's determined and will find a way to fit one of the big drums in the car. We return and dicker. Handsome as this drum is, the owner won't budge below thirty shillings. Bob tells him we'll think about it, and we drive on. After half-a-dozen more stops and chats with locals, we luck upon a man who says he'll show us a smaller drum at his house if we take him home.

Four of us pile into Zelda and bounce up a rutted track that looks as though no vehicle has driven it for months. When we reach the little compound, children playing outside are so scared of our car that one of them breaks into hysterical tears. Unfazed, our passenger hauls a drum outside, and bargaining starts at twenty-six shillings. After lengthy haggling, the owner won't go below twenty-three. Nathan tells us we're "the wrong color," and Bob says we'd best forget the deal. By now I'm dead-set on this drum, which I fell for at first sight. This one is too good to pass up no matter what the price. We agree to buy this drum for me and return for the big one for Bob. By one o'clock we're home again with two new keepsakes.

We rub down our drums with an oiled cloth and stand back to admire them. Bob's is nearly five feet tall and fourteen inches across the head. Mine is hip-high and eleven inches across. Each drum is a single hollowed-out log shaped with an hourglass indentation two-thirds of the way down. There's no decorative carving on the drum sides, but the wood has been rubbed to a deep brown, almost leather-like patina. A natural resin binds the goatskin heads three inches down from the top of each drum. A circle of blackened cow dung painted with resin centers the drumhead to cushion the player's fingertips. These drums can't be found in tourist shops and most likely not even in museums.

***

Joseph brings home a leg of goat from the town market. I sprinkle on tenderizer, thinking the meat might be tough. I roast it for a meal as good as any leg of lamb.

**

We didn't notice the heat much last year, but it's getting to us this season. Afternoon classes are grim. When I caught myself falling asleep at the head of the class last Friday, I took everyone outside under some trees for a reading lesson; I plan to do the same next week.

As for my own reading: I'm struggling through *Moby-Dick*.

**

We see our first African snake at home squirming around the hall as I step out of the bathtub and open the door. I let out a yelp, and Bob comes to my rescue with a club. After a few whacks, the snake wriggles its last, and Bob slides it out the door. It looks like a water snake, but Joseph tells us the next morning it's poisonous. I'm glad we found it before it found our bed.

**

Every day now a pint-sized villager delivers a twenty-ounce beer bottle of fresh milk to our door for seven cents. Zebu cows' milk isn't rich; it's more like skimmed milk, though it tastes better than reconstituted Danish powdered milk. I simmer the fresh milk for twenty minutes to kill parasites. We keep it in the fridge; to have real fresh milk for breakfast oatmeal is a luxury. From the top of the chilled milk a thin crust of cream, a tablespoon's worth, rises. In a week I collect half a cup and freeze ice cream.

164

European type dairy herds succeed in Kenya—hence the butter and cream we ration from the Mbeya shipment—but the only cattle found in these southern stretches are the humped, skinny Zebu. These animals thrive with the climate, vegetation, seasonal lack of water and most importantly they are not prey to the tsetse fly host for the parasite carrying sleeping sickness, fatal to humans and animals. These humped Brahmin type cattle provide stringy, watery meat and minuscule quantities of milk, but they flourish in the African savanna where they represent wealth and prosperity.

***

While we're discussing *Robinson Crusoe,* the word "Negro" comes up when man Friday enters Defoe's book. The boys understand that Negroes are former slaves in America. They pepper me with questions: Why does everyone hate Negroes in the States? Why do white people discriminate? The class jeers at me, whistling and scowling. Later, when I'm out of sight, I break into tears.

The next day I try to tell them discrimination exists everywhere, even here in East Africa where there is conflict between Africans and Asians. The boys disagree and contend discrimination exists only in America. I try to define propaganda: how other countries opposing America exaggerate minor mishaps, swaying Africans to think the entire U.S. bristles with racial strife. I try to use myself as an example, asking them if I felt superior, would I be teaching in Songea? In unison they reply, "You are just trying to deceive us."

***

Two schoolboys come to our house that afternoon and ask Bob, "Sir, why does the U.S. want to bomb us?" A radio news report has announced that a Coalition of Western Powers is seeking to quell the latest independence movements in Africa. Tanzania is a model for many countries that are still colonies on the brink of revolution. Tanzania has no money to send heavy arms but offers training for freedom fighters.

President Nyerere seems to be on good terms with the West; however, his two right-hand men, Kambona and Kawawa, face fully East. Last January when Nyerere was out of the capital, the army mutinied over pay and leadership. Kambona negotiated with the soldiers and emerged as a hero. To bolster his own power, he may have organized what could have been a coup. This month while Nyerere was visiting the northern Kigoma region of the country, Kambona put out news that he had discovered a letter warning the government of a plot by the "Western Powers," namely the U.S., to overthrow Tanzania. Kambona set up mass anti-American demonstrations in Dar to kick off the day of Nyerere's return. Nyerere, forced to step into the center of the uproar, used the event to preach "nation building"; he avoided the issue of a plot altogether. Nonetheless, the government now encourages anti-American demonstrations throughout Tanzania. Who knows what will happen at the scheduled march in our village.

* * *

I feel uneasy as I write "U.S.A." on letters home these days. We sense the anti-American furor in the wake of the alleged plot two weeks ago. We trust The White House and the BBC when we hear about documents being forged, but Africans cast a cold eye on "Europeans," i.e., any of us with ethnic ties to parts of Europe or the West. The African press says, "Look at the Cuban fiasco," "Look at what the U.S. is doing in Viet Nam." Security measures throughout the country cancel leaves for all civil servants, and word has it that ministry officials in Dar are practicing military maneuvers.

American aid continues to pour in while Tanzanians demonstrate against us. At a protest march in Lindi last Tuesday a young British teacher wrote signs in Swahili on his car in favor of the £35,000 worth of wheat that arrived on an American aid ship the previous day. He was immediately arrested, imprisoned and deported for gross misbehavior.

We suspect the anti-American issue has been devised to cover up trouble on Zanzibar that may mushroom into a world problem. The union of Tanganyika and Zanzibar appears to exist in name only. Tanzania represents the partnership of Communist-controlled Zanzibar and Tanganyika. The mainland still sympathizes with the West, while Zanzibar seems to be controlled by Chinese and East German Communists. There's also a Christian/Moslem conflict with Zanzibar long being a center for Islam while the Roman Catholics dominate most of the interior mainland. We hear of a British correspondent being tortured while on the island. A person may be deported from Zanzibar and sent to Dar, even though both are in the same country.

***

Tanzania is having a hard time uniting its people in a spirit of nation building under a five-year development plan. Nyerere continues to push for a grass roots spirit of *Ujamaa* (family-hood). He asks people to come together to form collectives for farming and marketing. He believes that the productive family will serve as a model for a productive nation. Unfortunately, most people don't like to work, and many resent being pushed around by TANU, the country's one political party. Keeping the people roused against something prevents them from complaining.

The saddest part of the story is that native folk are frightened. A huge plane flew over Songea yesterday. Suddenly everyone suspected it was a bomber. Our most competent African teacher, Mpogolo, fears this region will soon be invaded by the Portuguese from Mozambique.

***

We decide to make a second attempt to scale Matagoro Mountain, the big rock a mile from the school, before the rains start. I pull on a pair of slacks, unusual for me here where I wear skirts in deference to local custom, and we drive to the mission compound. Last year we tried to find the path. Everyone said it was so obvious we couldn't miss it, but this morning again we fail to find it and end up on the same trail we hiked last year.

We return to the car and climb the steep seven-mile track to the forest reserve. When we reach five thousand feet, fifteen hundred feet higher than the village, we're in cool air above timberline. Horseshoeing downward we don't see much of a forest, though seedling evergreens grow close together in nursery-like rows soon to be shipped out and planted for timber.

We wander alongside thousands of saplings in a miniature woodland. Alone, in absolute stillness, we peer down a ravine where a streamlet trickles through the valley's jungley undergrowth. I recall a silent canyon, remote yet not that far from Glenwood Springs in Colorado, where I picnicked with my aunt Margie years ago.

***

We've been watching the full moon rise for the past few nights. As we sit on our front steps, the horizon starts to glow sometime between 9 and 9:30. Soon the shining arc grows into a giant golden ball silhouetting the trees and hills. Stars glint in the darkness. The night is alive with crickets singing, and beetles hum in the shadows.

***

Last term I invited one of our African teachers and his wife for afternoon tea. I prepared orange muffins and waited over my steaming kettle, but my guests never appeared.

Today I gather up courage and invite his wife again along with the wife of another African teacher. By five o'clock my guess is they aren't coming but forty-five minutes later, they wheel their baby carriages up to the front porch. Their hair is neatly braided. They wear western style shirt-like blouses, wraparound *kanga* skirts and slip-on Bata sandals.

"I'm always happy when I eat bread," says Anna as I serve sliced homemade whole wheat bread with mulberry jelly. Jolla looks around my sitting room and spies a copy of *National Geographic* with an African mud and thatch dwelling on the cover. "Now what is that house on a magazine?" she asks as I show them the pictures of the African village at Disneyland in Anaheim, California.

They chuckle at the thought of Americans going to a fake African village to "play." Both women shake their heads, clicking their tongues against their teeth saying, "That is very strange."

Their two kids are well behaved as we chitchat. When they leave, Jolla stops to admire my parsley plants, and Anna questions, "Who is that I hear singing?" I can't hear anything, but as I cup my hands to both ears, I make out the faint click clicking of a bird's call.

* * *

It's common knowledge that one of our African teachers drinks away most of his evenings and spends time with local prostitutes. His wife, certain he is out for the night, invites strangers into her bed for company. We're surprised to hear that our headmaster has a couple of girls on his waiting list for an occasional fling. We are wrong in thinking a tribal moral code reins in such pursuits.

＊＊＊

On Thanksgiving Day no wind rustles through dry branches, no early snow blankets the soil, which has just given up its harvest. With summer rains the land is abloom in green as tropical sun warms the red clay soil.

We'll feast traditionally tonight with dinner at home. We've invited one of the Brits to share roast Kenyan pork—no turkey in these parts—flown in from Mbeya. I simmer dried apples that barely taste like applesauce. A South Dakota friend sent some paper Christmas decorations; I'll use them on the table. Our guest will bring over his record player and we'll listen to carols.

Just as I'm serving up the pudding, I hear a rap at the back door, and someone calls out, "*Hodi*?" (May I come in?) I crack the door open to a witchy wraith of a woman leaning on a crooked stick. She's wrapped in a dirty cloth with a rag around her head. She's muttering something in Swahili. Bob says, "*Kwa heri*" (good-bye) and shuts the door. The next day I mention the incident to Joseph, who laughs out loud, "Oh, *Memsab*, the old lady must have been very drunk and thought this was her house. You must never open the door when someone says '*Hodi*' at night."

＊＊＊

We raise a cheer when the U.S. and Belgium rescue prisoners from the Congo. But America continues to be condemned throughout Africa and the Eastern world for our intervention. Several African leaders held a meeting in Dar and disapproved of the rescue mission.

Most Africans feel there are two types of people here: nationalists and colonialists. The colonialists work to enrich themselves while the nationalists, the good guys, work to improve the continent. I used to think that recipients of U.S. aid felt kindly toward us.

* * *

We buck the odds and drive out to the Irish government/UN project at Mlale. We haven't been there since last July, and it's amazing to see the progress.

A year ago Mlale was a wilderness of low scrubby hills. Maize and tobacco fields spread out for acres. There are now one hundred and eighty settlers with their families, and each is allotted $2400 to get started!

When a settler arrives he receives a plot of ground and has two weeks to build a temporary mud or grass shelter. Later a team puts up a steel frame with an iron roof, and the family must make their own mud bricks to complete a permanent dwelling. From each cooperative farmer's two-acre tobacco plot, the first crop will be harvested next year. The Irish directors are working non-stop to get the project going; however, the young African who is training to take over spends most of his time dressed up in Western clothes, spinning around in a government Land Rover.

* * *

Bob heads for town today, and I hop in the car to keep him company. As we approach the village, we glimpse a tall man with glasses and a mustache wearing a short-sleeved white shirt, a black bow tie, long white sox with black cuffs, shiny black shoes—and a yellow tutu-like taffeta skirt that comes above his knees. Looks like part of a schoolgirl's dance recital costume that must have arrived here in a Good Will box.

DECEMBER, 1964

Here we are at the Courtney Hotel in Salisbury, Rhodesia. It's as though we're not in Africa.

As we cross the border from Tanzania into Zambia, we enter White Man's Land. Bumping along East African cow trails onto a paved roadway, we imagine we're in the American Midwest. We don't hit tar till Lusaka, but even the gravel roads here are wide as highways, with sixty-mile-an-hour speed limits. We see dozens of white faces behind steering wheels, and we hold onto our hats when a GMC pick-up passes us as we're doing seventy! Plus, we can drink water out of the tap!

The past days come back in a flash:

We leave Songea early Wednesday morning, and, thanks to tolerable roads, by mid-afternoon we arrive at Mbeya, our Mecca for mail and food flights. We overnight with Texan friends we met in Dar. We should hit the sack early, but we can't keep our mouths shut.

Back in Songea anti-American sentiments are nothing compared to what prevails here. In Mbeya our Texan missionary friends' kids were attacked while riding their bikes, and the back wall of their new church was set afire by arsonists.

***

You who believe that the United States is everyone's beloved big brother; that Americans working in underdeveloped countries are welcomed with open arms—hear ye: This is a LIE. Let's face up to the truth.

The same resentment is following Europeans who have settled in northern Tanzania. Many of these white folk have spent their lives developing coffee and sisal farms—until Tanganyika became independent and their farms were nationalized. They receive nominal payment for the land, but many are not allowed to hold onto personal possessions when they are ordered away.

China is now sending large shipments of heroin and opium into the Congo. Chinese military men are training the Tanzanian army, and a shipload of mysterious goods has come into Kenya from Russia along with many Russian citizens. The Chinese are sending agriculture advisors and plenty of farm equipment into Tanzania, but these officials don't seem to know about sisal and pyrethrum. Chinese tractors sit at depots like heaps of shiny junk.

***

We join the Great North Road, championed by Cecil John Rhodes founder of De Beers diamond mines, British empire builder and Rhodesia's namesake. Five hundred miles from Mbeya we stop at a ghostly place called Mkushi River. In a seedy hotel we share a dinner table with a veteran white African. He grew up in South Africa, farmed in East Africa and mined copper in Northern Rhodesia. When he was forced off the land, he picked up his shovel and started over again. He's nearly seventy, heading out to open a small copper mine. He told us his brother spent forty years working the soil in Kenya. When his land was nationalized, the mature pine trees he had been growing for timber were sold for a shilling each as firewood.

***

Civilization greets us two hundred miles south in Zambia's capital city. Lusaka is so new that the government buildings' fresh cement still looks wet. Zambia, the former Northern Rhodesia, achieved independence last October. We find department stores, almost a copy of J.C. Penney's, like nothing we've seen in Africa. White people sell hosiery and hats behind counters, fry burgers in snack bars and sell vegetables in the open market.

From now on we're in milk country and can stop for a pint, packaged in a triangular plastic carton, whenever we hanker for it. I'm taken by surprise when I see melons and peaches in the market. We buy a chunk of watermelon and slice it for lunch at the side of the road and spit seeds over a fence.

***

We depart early in the afternoon for Kariba Dam in the gorge of the Zambezi River on the southern Rhodesian border. The vertigo-inducing gigantic semicircular structure has created the largest man-made lake on the planet. Fishermen and bird watchers travel there for holidays. At the present only the southern power station is completed and sends current to both countries, with heavy loads going to the copper mining area north of Lusaka.

We overnight in a chalet camp at the side of the lake. The motel-like spot offers mountain-cabin huts complete with mini-kitchens. We've brought sliced ham and fruit for supper and enjoy a sundown swim in the lake. Our neighbors in the chalet next door invite us for a drink, and we chat with them a couple of hours. These folks, Afrikaners, have made a killing on maize and cattle and are living high in Zambia. They natter on about their black African countrymen. We cringe when we hear this.

The next morning we sip coffee with the chalet's manager, a man in his sixties who farmed sixteen years in Kenya and two years in Tanganyika. He and his wife give us pointers, and now we can hardly wait to drive into the other U.S.A.—the Union of South Africa.

On a winding dirt road out from Kariba Dam, a guinea fowl soars straight up in front of us. We're moving too fast to miss him, and he smacks the center of our windshield with a dead clunk. His weight, no more than a big chicken, impacts us like a boulder; we skid to a halt. After our last windshield fiasco our laminated glass doesn't splinter in our faces, but it caves in on us. Two hundred miles from Salisbury, with no chance for quick repair, we plug on. Now the road is paved and so smooth that Bob can't resist zipping up to sixty, though the wind pushes the smashed glass inward. For the next four hours we take turns bolstering the crunched windshield till our triceps turn into knots.

***

Now at the Courtney Hotel in Salisbury, we rub our sore arms, dress up and reward ourselves with an extravagant dinner. We down a bottle of South African wine with lamb chops and tuck into an ice cream dessert. We dance till my feet blister in dress-up shoes. I think I look good in my gray Jantzen knit skirt and sweater, but when I glance at the women with bee-hived dos and chiffon cocktail dresses, I know I've just come in from the bush.

***

Bob deals with the car this afternoon and has a long talk with someone who lives across from the hotel. This guy came to Southern Rhodesia from Ireland three years ago. When independence comes to Rhodesia, he feels it will become another chaotic Congo. As independence spreads, he'll continue to migrate south. He says South African whites are involved in an experiment diametrically opposed to what's happening in the U.S.A. with civil rights. This "apartheid" or "separate development" stuff is getting to us!

In Salisbury we obtain South African visas and revive Zelda. The Portuguese embassy informs us it will take two days to process visas for Lourenço Marques. The wait increases our uneasiness about having a Mozambique stamp on our passport since Tanzania is violently anti-Portuguese, so we give it up.

***

Tuesday we set out for Fort Victoria and the Zimbabwe ruins. Near the Fort torrential rain tempts us to call it quits, but we press on.

We walk over a red dirt path and climb thirteen hundred feet, picking our way through rubble. We come to a stone citadel built by the Zimbabwe people dating back to perhaps seven hundred AD. Some historians think this may be the ancestral home of the Queen of Sheba.

We observe a circular gray stone enclosure, where ancient Shona tribes used no mortar but fit stones together to form massive walls. We step through an opening and wander around the acropolis now strewn with crumbling walls, patches of grass and rock piles. We try to imagine the living spaces that must have housed hundreds in this now silent city where trees and bushes grow.

***

We stay the night in a rest camp at the ruins and chat with the museum director whom we met in Songea. She insists we stay for tea and come back for dinner. In her cottage she pours us small glasses of old sticky Port, then serves a typical meat stew and rice that her house steward has prepared. We continue listening to Africa's growing pains and Zimbabwe's history. "I simply cannot find capable aides for the museum," she says.

Rhodesia is in a tight spot. The white minority government is struggling with Britain for independence, and Britain is determined to turn the country over to the blacks. The whites see the Congo's turmoil as a sign of what's to come.

* * *

We drive across the Limpopo River into the Union of South Africa. After living around scrubby *shambas,* we relish the vast cultivated fields. Following plenty of rain, the landscape glows. Most of the homes are modest and immaculate. White people appear to be large and ruddy, the blacks charming. Black men dress in overalls, shirts and shoes, and the women wear Western-style calico dresses and headscarves in contrast to most of our village folk wrapped in black cloth or kangas. I'd love to converse with the South Africans we see, but English is hard for them. Most whites here speak Afrikaans, and the blacks speak different Bantu dialects.

* * *

One hundred and fifty miles from Pretoria we settle into a motel with individual rondavels (round mud hut-like cabins with thatched roofs). The bedspread is a multicolored quilt, and there's a Gideon Bible on the dresser. The owners, a seventy-ish Afrikaans couple, have a tidy garden, and their little generator starts put-putting at precisely 6:30. Our basic hotel roast beef dinner plus our room come to $4.25.

* * *

I need to buy new clothes. The elastic is out on most of our undies; my tennis shoes are holey and the zipper is about to go on my slacks. We'll have to disguise everything we buy; there's a strict embargo on all South African goods. If customs officers discover South African purchases, they'll burn them at the Tanzanian border.

＊

This "U.S.A." is a wealthy old lady. Except for petroleum, she's pretty much self-sufficient. The rest of the world needs her for gold and diamonds. She doesn't seem to care about the bad press she's getting. She believes she's right and strong enough to stick to Kruegerrands and De Beers.

We keep hearing that apartheid means separation, not segregation. Interracial marriages are officially forbidden. If this sounds cruel, at the very least there seems to be order and progress, outwardly more so here than elsewhere on the continent. Black folk here have their own schools, communities, and a place in the government.

We stop at a supposedly authentic Bantu village, which we learn is a tourist trap. Children shadow us asking for money, and some old ladies hawking beaded items curse me in Zulu when I claim their prices are too high. In the local paper we read that the minimum wage for South Africans is one hundred forty shillings per week; the minimum wage in Tanzania is one hundred shillings a month.

＊

As we approach Johannesburg, I remember when my high school drama class listened to the record of Maxwell Anderson and Kurt Weill's musical *Lost in the Stars*. Those lyrics, "Black man go to Johannesburg, never come back, never come back," haunt me now as I think of Africans who seek work in the city but feel displaced when they sing:

But I've been walking through the night and the day
Till my eyes get weary and my head turns gray
And sometimes it seems maybe God's gone away
Forgetting the promise that we heard him say.

Joburg's a hyperactive city not equipped to welcome tourists. It takes us five hours to find a hotel room. So many nonresidents work in the inner city that most tourist lodgings have become residence hotels. If you're unwilling to stay a month and eat all meals on the premises, forget about it—there's no room at the inn. We end up at one of the bigger hotels downtown, shelling out more than we can afford just to stay a couple of nights.

Joburg is bigger than Denver, but it's not New York. In spite of its size and hubbub, it's clean. We're told black Africans aren't allowed to live within the city limits. Things weren't always this way, but as crime increased, rules and regulations finger-pointed the blacks out of town. On the other hand, we tour a couple of public universities where blacks can attend free of charge. Blacks are also eligible to receive free medical care from the state, whereas whites must pay for these services.

After flopping into our hotel room, we slip on city duds and set off on a spree. I purchase tennis shoes and cotton undies. I look for a wash-and-wear dress. We pause for ice cream. We change into new togs and hike to an early showing of the Burton/O'Toole *Becket*. The theatre is so baroquely ornate I feel I'm in Milan or San Francisco, though we shell out only one dollar each for our seats.

Later, dining near the theatre, we revel in T-bone steaks done up with mushroom sauce and whisky flambé. There's a small dance band in the corner, so we get plenty of exercise.

Close to midnight as we make our way down the restaurant stairs, I think I see a familiar face. Woozy after the wine, I nearly trip over our teacher buddies, Gil and Mike. We can't believe we've come face to face with our bush home pals here more than fifteen hundred miles south.

***

We depart Joburg too late the next morning to make Durban in a day but finally call it quits in Pietermaritzburg. At a small motel we get our money's worth as I do a week's worth of laundry in the tub, wash my hair and bathe like a queen. Bob spends a couple of hours drinking beer and chewing the fat with the motel manager. He has trouble defending American foreign policy with the manager, a Swiss immigrant, who doesn't have much good to say about the way we Yanks think we own Europe. A few people we meet over here are pro-American, but most think we're a bunch of goons.

***

In Durban the next morning, we go right to work looking for lodgings. Again we can't find an affordable room, so we push on to one of the outlying towns. Bob says, "Whoa!" twenty miles south of Durban where it looks like Redondo or Manhattan Beach near LA where he lived for three years. Unfortunately, we can't find a vacancy there either; it's the holiday season. In a fit of desperation I gesture to a friendly-looking gent on the street and ask him where we might find an inexpensive room.

"Come in and ask my wife if we can't do something for you," he says. We follow him two blocks to a modest bungalow, where his wife greets us with a cup of tea. He and his family have driven down from Joburg for the holiday. They've just arrived and are still unpacking, but they say they'll gladly rent us a spare room. Not only do they give us a room; they insist that we stay for tea and supper. The dad's an electrician and the mom's a bookkeeper; their two girls are in high school.

"Hope you don't mind eating mealie meal, it's our national dish," the mom says as she pours a thin stream of what looks like white cornmeal into a pot of boiling water. As the ground corn cooks to a stiff porridge, she fries spicy sausages and makes a thin gravy with the drippings. "This is our everyday rice and beans sort of food," she says as she spoons the thick grits-like mush onto our plates and tops it with sausage and a drizzle of gravy. We're thrilled to be out of a hotel for a night.

"We cook mealie meal for breakfast, too," says the dad who claims the best morning dish in the world is a bowl of mush with milk and sugar. Bob diplomatically asks about the "separate development" scheme of the current government. Our host replies, "You know, I'm so caught up in making an honest living and keeping my home in order I can't even think beyond the next football score."

* * *

Onward and northward the next morning we drive past sugar cane fields and the beach. The Indian Ocean water is turquoise at times, compared to the gray-green of the California Pacific. We stop for a stroll to gaze at the horizon.

Back in Durban we're lucky enough to locate a hotel, stop for a hot dog and mosey into an Indian market where curry powder and ground spices, heaped in oversized dishpans, wait to be weighed out in paper packets. I long to cook a shrimp and coconut curry with fresh tomatoes.

We wander to the beachside aquarium, watch rickshaw boys pulling tourists, and settle for grilled steak with cheap, local wine. You'd think I'd find good fish here on the coast, but the locals are set on steak.

* * *

Folks we talk to beg us to consider settling here. South Africa needs teachers. It's a gorgeous country, and whites are trying their damnedest to get more Europeans to emigrate. If we were totally broke we'd stay, but our American passports are too precious to jeopardize.

***

For two days Zelda eats up miles of barren countryside speckled with Bantu reserves. This vast territory, the Transkei, is under black African control. We stay a night in the government town of Umtata. After we take a room in the only hotel, I find the communal bathrooms have wads of toilet paper on the floor, soap-scummy sinks and brown crusted toilets. I wonder if I can "hold it" all night. Although I know it's right that both blacks and whites are staying in the hotel, I'm squeamish.

***

It hardly seems possible that today is the last Sunday before Christmas, and we're about to pass another Yule in Africa. Most South Africans are Christian, but it's their summer vacation, school holiday time. Everyone heads for the beach. Families camp in trailers or tents along the coasts. Beach hotels are booked, and prices are up everywhere. No one talks about Christmas. We haven't seen one lighted tree in a house window.

***

We hug the coast from Durban to Port Elizabeth. We check out a few hotels; they're all full. Someone suggests we try an apartment house across the street. I soon learn that an "apartment house" here means a guesthouse that doesn't serve meals, while a "house of flats" is what we call an apartment house.

Ken Long's guesthouse looks A-OK but expensive. We ask if there's a campsite nearby and are directed to a place outside of town. The campground looks like an outdoor flophouse for migrant workers. We decide we'd rather sack out alongside the highway. Bob cuts some willow branches for a makeshift pup tent with our sleeping bags' tops. We're filthy and famished when we bolt down a dry hamburger at a drive-in.

The guesthouse couple has second thoughts and scouts us out at the drive-in. Ken says, "If you've got sleeping bags, why don't you roll them out in one of our rooms? You can have a bath and morning coffee. We'll give you the lot for ten bob." I pull money out of my pocket, and we follow him back. Apparently, he and his wife had heard rumors about the campground and decided they couldn't think of letting us stay there.

After a hot bath, tea and cakes lead to our visit with the Longs till after midnight. Farmers in the barren Karoo north of the Cape, for years they raised sheep and goats. When their children left for school, they sold the farm and bought the guesthouse here in Port Elizabeth.

From Ken, a native English speaker, we learn about the divisiveness and resentment between English speakers and Afrikaners. For that matter, there are three groups of white people in South Africa: the Jews, the British and the Afrikaners. Today it seems as though Afrikaners, descendents from the pioneer Dutch who settled here in the seventeenth century, are gaining the upper hand in government policy matters. This makes the Brits burn; many consider the Afrikaners rowdy brutes. Be that as it may, Ken and Barb are the first white people we've spoken to who sympathize with black and colored Africans.

Ken and Barb wait till dark and check to make sure all windows are shut and doors locked before speaking openly. Sometimes they use French phrases like *Ce n'est pas juste,* or *Nous avons peur des avocats.* How can anyone, they ask us, say that non-whites go in one side of the post office and whites go in another. They speak about the lack of training and shortage of teachers here; education seems to be way behind that in the U.S. Schools are overcrowded, many teachers have only two years of college and texts are often outdated. Before we go off to bed we want to grasp their hands and sing "Kumbaya."

***

Near the beach city of George we take a day at the High Gate Ostrich Farm, where we get a crash course in the history of ostrich feathers. To top things off, Bob bronc-rides an ostrich's saddled back, grabbing its skinny neck carefully not to get pecked by its hooked bill. We taste scrambled ostrich egg and buy a feather duster.

***

From George it's fair sailing to Cape Town, where we find lodgings ten miles from the city in a monstrous old home turned into a rooming house for university students, and during holiday seasons, tourists. It looks like an old folks' home sort of hotel, but we get bed and breakfast for $3.50 a day.

***

Sunday we follow the curve of the cape to Table Mountain. As we approach we think of western Colorado's Grand Mesa, the world's largest flat-topped mountain. Way back in the Grand Valley, we knew our directions because the Mesa was east. Here in Cape Town sheer rock juts up as a natural fortress at the southern sea's edge. We park Zelda and walk over wild-flower-dotted meadow inclines to gaze at gigantic boulders buttressing deep ravines. A rusty funicular cable car creeps above stone cliffs, but I'm not about to put my foot in it.

At the base of the mountain, the beach looks inviting, but a cold breeze keeps swimmers away.

* * *

Tuesday morning while Bob's having Zelda's gearbox checked at a filling station, he meets Nick, a Frieslander-Dutchman, who's worked in South Africa for eleven years. He's in his early thirties, single and on vacation here, too. We glom together like three bugs in a rug, all of us eager for company in away-from-home surroundings. German-looking blue-eyed wavy-blond Nick offers us a warm Hollander welcome.

He invites us to lunch at a little pub in a nearby hotel. All's lovely in the warm December holiday mood of an afternoon. We munch ham sandwiches and sip beer—till two boisterous guys join the party and coax us to live it up more than we're used to. We blab for a couple of hours as we share stories, and of course pretty soon I'm talking food. One of the burly guys insists on opening some South African bubbly. I ooze with excitement, forgetting Bob and Nick have already downed two quarts of beer. Mr. Football has oodles of rands to blow, and by four o'clock, the five of us have gone through five bottles of sparkling. I know, I know. I should've stopped after the third glass.

It will be a long time before Bob and I indulge in any champagne. I don't feel bad. I'm not soused, but as for the other beer and bubbly boys—well, I won't go into detail. Suffice it to say we come straight back to our tourist home, fall into bed, and for the next few hours I do a lot of mopping up.

* * *

I light out alone by bus for the city the next morning to walk through some of the old department stores. I dream of finding a slice of fruit cake but only end up with a handful of fresh seeded Muscat raisins. I can't buy anything now, but I want to feel the pulse of this city that reminds me of downtown Denver with its big Sears and Daniels & Fisher stores. I want to be a part of it for a while as I imagine the Dutch who built Cape Town right around the time New York City was Nieuw Amsterdam. We're relatives from a similar rootstalk, now branching apart.

***

This afternoon I sit down in the breakfast room with the landlady. Right off she starts in about the "Cape Coloreds." She repeats what appears to be the general consensus down here: "The white race is committing suicide. We're teaching our people to use birth control. The rest of the world says, 'Have more babies. We'll get the West by force of numbers.'"

I ask the landlady about one of her colored maids, a sweet-looking girl I've passed in the hall. The landlady tells me her name is Wonder. She's twenty-nine and has given birth to fourteen children, each with a different father. She doesn't know who the fathers are. She hasn't kept her children. She gives them away to whoever will take them. The landlady claims girls like Wonder are taught to have as many children as they can. It isn't a question of religious teaching; it's social indoctrination—and I feel the landlady is trying to indoctrinate me!

Almost everyone we talk to in S.A. believes apartheid is a temporary phenomenon.

The locals tell us that if a black African is given a position as a foreman over black workers he'll push them harder than a white foreman. They say, "You give a black man a blanket and eight out of ten will sell it to buy liquor. You send food to starving black kids and Papa sits at home saying, 'Now I don't have to work, let the kids go to school for their breakfast.'"

Should we teach others our way of thinking when their ideas oppose ours? As I listen to white people yammer, I stand back and wonder how I can do any good. I'm supposed to be a teacher; I'm supposed to know how to ask questions that will point to the truth, but I don't know how to respond to these racists. Plus, I'm a guest in their country. Are they blind-sided by Cape Town's False Bay, where they cling to a meager viewpoint?

* * *

Bob and Nick have recovered from Tuesday's bacchanal, and we've invited Nick to join us on Christmas afternoon. I order a barbecued chicken, and buy tomatoes, strawberries and bread rolls. Nick has a dry ice bag, and promises to bring a block of ice cream.

As it turns out, we have a lovely Christmas. We picnic in the sun high on Table Mountain. We spread our feast on a slab of rock near a grassy patch on a headland above the ocean. We're nestled beside a small rise, a windbreak, and in the warmth of midday we have to eat the ice cream first. We're far above any spray, but the tinge of salt water fills the air here where the continent ends.

That evening the landlady surprises her guests with a buffet supper that turns into a holiday party. We heap plates with turkey, stuff ourselves with mini–mince pies, and dance through a stack of Glenn Miller records. At midnight we skip off the dance floor since we have an early start to make six hundred miles the next day.

* * *

During the miserable drive in unbearable heat we pinch each other and take turns at the wheel to stay awake. The land swims like a mirage, desolate, desert-like. We stop to wash our faces in the cold water of a sheep trough.

In Kimberly we stop at a diamond mine, where museum photos look like scenes of the California gold rush. Heat presses us through the Karoo till we emerge onto high veldt and sweater-up in cool Transvaal breezes.

We room with Beth and Tim near Johannesburg (we met Beth's mom at the guest house). They mow their lawn and plant flowerbeds. Their children go to Scouts and take music lessons. I help with supper and run a load of laundry. All of a sudden racial questions seem far away, and this suburb of a city where many black Africans have lost their identity seems like Grand Junction, where in 1959 we had only three black students in a high school of fifteen hundred.

* * *

In a theatre queue I strike up a conversation with a woman behind me. She and her husband have lived in Joburg all their lives. They end up sitting next to us. *My Fair Lady* is perfectly "loverly." Bob and I watch with tears dripping down our cheeks. After the show my new friend and her husband, treat us to pastry and coffee. They invite us to spend a day with them, but by now we're beginning to feel like a couple of pick-ups and tell them we'd best be on our way.

* * *

This morning at the American Embassy in Pretoria two letters wait for us. One is from Colorado Congressman Wayne Aspinall. His letter suggests that if we make sacrifices we'll achieve goals that are good for all mankind. This sounds laudable, but it isn't true. Bob and I, along with countless volunteers, are making sacrifices, but we're NOT achieving goals. We're losing faster than we're winning. We're beginning to wonder if our high-sounding foreign policy isn't being dreamed up in stuffy Washington offices. Congressman Aspinall should spend a month in the African bush.

By afternoon we cross back into Southern Rhodesia and again pass women hauling weighty loads of firewood on their heads.

On New Year's Eve day at Victoria Falls the Zambezi River drops over the world's largest waterfall on the border of Zambia and Southern Rhodesia. We plan to treat ourselves to a bit of festivity at a swanky hotel near the falls, even though we're staying at a bare-bones rest camp in the village.

This morning I notice three weird looking bites on my left ankle, and after a few scratches they start to ooze. I wipe yellow goo off my foot all morning, and by early afternoon my ankle is swollen, the bites have blistered, and I feel light-headed. At the same time Bob finds red welts on his arms and neck. We think it best to find a doctor in Livingston. The doctor doesn't know whether we've been visited by a scorpion or a spider, but it's more than a mosquito. Our New Year's Eve fund ends up in the doctor's pocket. By evening we're done in by whatever the insects have donated to our body chemistry. We share a tin of baked beans and see 1964 fade away before eight-thirty.

January, 1965

We buzz along good roads all the way home through Zambia and in Tanzania where the rains are behind schedule. We don't meet washed-out bridges or seasonal potholes. After ten thousand miles on the road, we shout hooray when we see our little yellow house. The grass is taller and the forest greener than when we left. Our three hens are still scratching, and neat rows in our garden show us that Joseph has been busy.

***

The school term begins with a thud. French is now an extra, which means I teach evenings, lunch hours and Sundays. One of my English classes looks like a joy, and the other a pain. Both are grouped according to ability, with a chasm of difference between the two. Group A is easily three times as quick and imaginative as Group B.

I'm planning to divide my students into seven committees of five for panel discussions. Each will have a chairman and each member will be allowed to choose a topic such as hunting and fishing, tribal dances, trades and vocations. I'm hoping to move away from stodgy written and memorized speeches. The boys are supposed to read a simplified version of *of Animal Farm*. I don't know how I'm going to avoid heated political discussions when we discuss it.

***

My student Michael Kambona writes an essay about his childhood:

My home is Kalembo in Tukunyu district near Mbeya. This is a small valley surrounded by a range of Bundali mountains and the Kalambo River joins the Songwe River which is a border between Tanganyika and Malawi. At the foot of these mountains there are temperate forests where women get firewood and children enjoy the wild fruits.

I remember when I was about four or five, I was very inquisitive. I sometimes asked myself from where my mother got me. These sort of questions occupied my mind at a considerable rate. In 1950 my mother gave birth to a girl child. I asked her from where she got it. She said babies were available in large numbers at Kalambo River. I absolutely believed her because I knew not any way by which one could get a baby. Then I asked her where she got me. From Kalambo River was the answer. Her answers gave me anxiety. My head was full of plans. I had a plan of getting one baby from that river. I asked a couple of my friends to accompany me to Kalambo River which was a few yards from my home. We waited for babies at the riverbank but all that was in vain.

In the evening, the family of a Mandali likes to sit around the fire. During this time they do not sit on chairs. Instead they sit on stools. Only father, mother and their daughters are allowed to sit on the stools. The boys sit on mats. During my childhood I was rather clumsy. Sometimes I sat on the stool. When my mother saw me she grew angry. I could not ask her why I was forbidden to do so, because I was afraid of strokes. As I grew bigger and bigger, I happened to query her why I had no right to use the stool. The answer was simply because I would then be as important as my father. It does not matter for girls because they will one day leave their family and marry, then they will be important no longer. But when sons get married, they still have some dependence on their father.

In my village there is a forested area. Wandali people call it Masheto. This is a place where pagans go to pray to their supernatural forces, like our ancestor Jumbe who died many years ago. There are many kinds of fruits growing wildly. My mother told me stories about them. She said they are not edible. If one ate, he or she would automatically die. If he or she did not die, he or she would give birth to an armless child. These stories made me respect Mascheto.

Wandali dislike fights. Buka (my brother) and I used to fight. Our mother was not happy with our fights. In order to avoid them, she told us stories of people who fought and when they died, they led disgraceful lives. She said our forefathers who died long ago are displeased when they see us fight. When we shall die, they will not welcome us into the resting souls. When we talked about people who died years back, our mother said the souls of the dead people could come to our beds and frighten us when we fell asleep.

***

I've smuggled a tin of lobster from South Africa. I open it this evening for lobster bisque with real cream, and brandy.

I'm into yet another spree of Indian cooking and have paid a couple more visits to Indian ladies in town. I learn as much about their lives as I do about food. It's Ramadan when Moslems are forbidden to eat from dawn to sunset. However, they have huge meals with numerous special dishes each evening.

I prepare my first jar of Indian oil pickles from green mango and carrots. I show it to the ladies and ask if I've made the pickles right. They don't understand and think I mean for them to take the pickles. When they bring me back the empty jar, I ask where the pickles are and try to explain that one jar is all I have. Finally, we breach the language barrier, and they return my pickles to their jar. I don't think anymore about it till I realize I may have made a blunder taking back what appeared to be a gift. I'll make a box of coconut macaroons and brownies and drive them to town this afternoon.

***

Bob reminds me to dust flour off my nose before I dash out the door to class. He wipes my tears when I spill turmeric into the egg whites I'm saving for a Lady Baltimore cake.

***

Mournful music in homage to Winston Churchill has saturated the radio waves today.

***

As we read *The Hunchback of Notre Dame* in class this morning, we come across a sentence describing a frightened girl whose face is ghastly white and whose lips are blue. To explain this to the boys, I tell them how I might look if the color were drained from my face, leaving my lips the color of my pale lavender blouse. One boy raises his hand and says, "We'd like to see it; may we try to frighten you someday?"

***

This weekend marks Vic, June and Hare's birthdays. I take advantage of a load of cheap coconuts and set to work on an Indian dinner party for the whole crew:

Ground Beef and Potato Samosas with Coconut Yogurt Chutney
Dal Soup
Chicken Curry; Meatball Curry
Coriander and Tamarind chutneys
Brown Beans and Cooking Bananas in Coconut Milk

Chapatis and Rice
Banana Cake with Carmel Icing

I make bowls of coconut milk by prying the meat from the shells and grating it finely. We squeeze the grated coconut in warm water and strain out the coconut fiber that then tastes like sawdust while the sweet nutty flavor stays in the liquid. I wonder how many hundreds of garlic cloves Joseph has peeled for the dinner. There must be some valuable health ingredients in garlic. Asians say it aids digestion. No one says our meal is too spicy. By now we have a yen for Asian food and can sit down to a plate of rice pilaf with korma the same way Americans enjoy spaghetti and meatballs.

FEBRUARY 1965

Today and tomorrow mark the Moslem holiday of Eid ul-Fitr, which means, for us, a day off from school.

This morning we drive to Peramiho to make dental appointments for Friday and chat with the Brother who will mend a pair of Bob's slacks in the tailor's shop. On the way back to Songea we offer a lift to a woman and her young child. We're shocked when she takes two shillings out of her purse to pay us for the ride. Of course we don't accept her money, but the offer is a first.

* * *

I've just made marshmallows. I didn't know it was possible to make them at home, but I found a recipe in my mom's old copy of *Granddaughter's Inglenook Cookbook.* The marshmallows are square instead of round and as nice as bought ones. We want to float them in cocoa or toast them over a campfire, but it's enough simply to bite into their sweet fluff.

Marshmallows

1 tablespoons unflavored gelatin (one envelope)

4 tablespoons cold water

7 oz. (1 cup) sugar

4 fl. oz. (½ cup) boiling water

1 teaspoons vanilla

1. Lightly oil a 4 ½ inch by 8 ½ inch loaf tin.

2. Sprinkle gelatin over cold water in bottom of deep mixing bowl. Allow it to sponge. Add a drop of food coloring if desired.

3. Combine sugar and boiling water in medium saucepan. Swirl to dissolve, cover briefly then wash down any sugar crystals on side of pan with wet pastry brush. Boil to soft-ball stage.

4. Slowly pour boiling syrup over softened gelatin, beating-it in with a fork. Continue to beat with rotary or electric mixer until stiff and cool (about 10 minutes). Add vanilla, beat to combine, scoop and smooth into oiled tin. Mixture will seem sticky but will set with a tissue-like surface.

5. When set, loosen edges and turn out onto board coated with powdered sugar. Cut into squares and dust with more powdered sugar. Makes 36 one-inch square marshmallows.

Note: add a drop of food coloring to the softening gelatin for pastel colored sweets.

***

On a rainy day Bob starts sniffling, and now my throat is scratchy. Does aspirin do any good for a cold? Bob says yes since it helps the body fight the virus, but I think it only keeps down fever and relieves aches. I've decided not to take aspirin if I don't have either a headache or a fever. I've been smearing Mentholatum on my neck, wrapping up in a scarf, gargling with salt water and drinking all the tea I can hold. Bob is swallowing aspirin. Marie, our nurse neighbor, says it would be good to take Pyrabenzamine and aspirin together.

***

Noel and Maisie come for dinner Saturday night. I prepare trifle, a favorite English dessert—it's no mere trifle! It's a combination of sponge cake spread with raspberry jam, soaked in sweet sherry and covered with custard, whipped cream and toasted almonds. A bit of Mbeya cream transforms custard made from Bird's powder and the raspberry jam comes from Yugoslavia.

***

Once again it's pineapple season. I've been making fresh pineapple juice by putting the flesh through my meat grinder and pressing the pulp in a sieve. I get a cup and a half of juice from a small pineapple, but it's heaps better than canned pineapple juice. I remember when I thought Dole from a can was exotic.

I also don't think I'll ever go out of my way to eat papaya. We call them pawpaws here and for weeks on end they're our only fruit. They're as big as footballs, mushy, bland, and edible only with a good squeeze of lime.

***

Bob goes to the dentist at Peramiho and sits like a ramrod while an elderly nun in a heavy gray habit and thick glasses works a foot-pumped drill like you'd see in a museum. It's a grind, like drilling through hardwood with a hand-turned bit, but he's thankful for the breakthrough and toothache relief. Our Sister dentist then takes out pliers like one of Grandpa's horse-tooth pullers. She yanks out a decayed baby tooth that I still have at 23. When I smile I now have a gap that will need to be patched, but it's healthier than a rotten spot.

***

Last week when June poured kerosene into her stove tank, some fuel spilled on the dirt floor. She struck the match to light the burner and her adopted African son, Wamedi, went up in flames. Hare threw himself down on top of the child to smother the blaze, but the boy was badly burned. They rushed him to Peramiho on their motorbike, where he spent two weeks in intensive care. The treatment may well leave him without a scar. Again we stand in awe of Paramiho, a microcosm of technology in the bush.

***

We're hosting our first overnight house guest this Valentine's Day. Don, the TEA administrative assistant, is on safari to check in on all of us. He planned to stay with Mike and Vic, but their house is full with Hare, June and Wamedi.

We're glad to have Don. It was his apartment we stayed in over the Christmas holiday of '63 while we were in Kampala. He's lanky and still single. He finished a Master's in administration at Princeton and travels with only a backpack. He spent twenty-seven months hitchhiking alone around the world a few years ago and wrote the book, *Walk The Wide World.*

To celebrate the day I made heart-shaped sugar cookies and pink marshmallows for everyone.

***

Today Bob heard his history students have scored a never-before-achieved eighty percent pass on their Cambridge exam. The results make for a terrific morale boost. Masudi leads the pack with a "Hip, hip, hooray" and "We are overjoyed and grateful for your learning, Sir" as Bob walks into class.

* * *

This must be lizard season. We have baby lizards scrambling all over the walls. I used to think lizards were scary, but here we're glad to have them as fly-and-mosquito eaters. Some hatchlings are only about the size of a bobby pin.

* * *

These days it's so hot we can hardly drag ourselves around. Late mornings and afternoons are miserable; we hope for rain to cool off the evening. We usually collapse for a few minutes after lunch. Getting off the couch to face the sweaty two-o'clock brood is the hardest chore of the day.

* * *

I think I'm going back to school to become an accountant, so I can take a four-dollar taxi ride to work and buy a Ford Galaxie. This teaching business at fifty cents an hour is for the ostriches. Still, I wouldn't take a taxi if there were a bus, and I'm happy with Zelda. Conspicuous consumption in America is going to be the hardest thing for me to return to. If our students could taste the leftovers that go down Grand Junction's garbage disposals every day, Songea Secondary School would have a banquet.

* * *

I'm so sick of being called a "neocolonialist" and an "imperialist aggressor" that I turn off the radio news. Bob helps me see why we're losing the propaganda war in this part of the world. Africans no longer want to hear America was once a British colony. That happened too

199

long ago, and current events are against us. Our U.S. racial strife is shooting us in the feet in Africa.

When the Tanzanian Broadcasting Company reports Malcom X's death, I'm saddened and grateful his assassin isn't a white guy. The news story begins, "In America they shoot black men down like cats."

***

One of my students gives a speech, "The Role of Homosexuality in African Family Life." My eyes bug. He tells how in homosexual love two boys or two girls meet in secret. They cut their arms a bit and become, as we would say, "blood brothers."

MARCH 1965

It's strange to hear the schoolboys speak English outside of class. The Cambridge test results in English have been so poor that we're encouraging our students to use English both in and outside of class. It will be a game for a day or two, and if it continues it will be good practice.

One of my classes is composing essays about the concept of maturity. Students choose one thing they consider difficult for a young adult. One boy writes a discourse on how hard it is for him to control his "sexual sensations" and avoid intercourse with the girls. Zuberi writes more formally about "Marriage Customs":

My district, Masasi (near the coast), is inhabited by natives who are either Christians or Moslems. The marriage customs in both religions are similar. When a man sees a girl who attracts him and wants to marry her, he faces his uncle or brother, usually a chief or elderman, and explains his difficulties. The chief on the next morning goes to the girl's parents and tells them what the young man has told him. Although it isn't necessary, it is advisable for the chief to face the parents before they wake up in the morning. If the talk between them is successful, a dowry is assessed. The dowry is divided into three sections. There is the money which the fiancé pays to the parents on the first instance he sees the girl publicly which is known as Hodi. Hodi *is equivalent to the knocking on the door by Europeans, but in our case it is to let the parents of the girl know of a man's presence as a fiancé. The sum of money paid for* Hodi *is rarely over ten shillings. The second section of the dowry is divided among the girl's brothers and sisters together with the uncles. This is called* Kitambo *(short amount of time) and allows the fiancé to be a member of the girl's family. The sum of money is very rarely over one hundred shillings. The money is divided amongst the girl's relatives so that when the girl later decides to divorce her husband they may help to repay the dowry. The last section of the dowry includes the money for house expenses and clothes for the bride.*

When all this has been decided, the Christian community goes to register the marriage to a priest who announces it in the church for three weeks to ask for anyone who has objections to the marriage. During the last week the man's and the girl's parents engage them- selves in the preparation of pombe (native beer), *which is made of millet or cassava flour mixed with yeast prepared also from millet. A day before the marriage is spared for native dances. The dances continue for the whole night up to the morning of the wedding day. The bride and the bridegroom are carried to the church in two chairs tied to two strong poles and these poles are carried by two pairs of men, one pair in front, the other at the back. The carriers take their duty in turns. After the procession in the church the marriage is complete.*

The Moslem community is a bit different. When the dowry is assessed, a "sheikh" who is responsible for marriages is informed of the event. He fixes a date and from then the parents prepare them- selves for the marriage. On the wedding day the bride stays inside the wedding house with other women while the bridegroom stays outside with the men. Usually the men stay in the open air during the dry seasons and under verandas during the rainy seasons. With the sheikh's direction, the men say some prayers and then the sheikh says a prayer to unite the bride and bridegroom, although they are at separate places. After the process, since Moslems consider pombe *illegal, they have a big feast of rice and the meat of a goat or chicken with a drink, sweet, unfermented beer known as togwa. The ceremony in this case doesn't take long because Moslems don't like native dances."*

***

As I leave my second period class this morning, Bob calls out to me from the school office saying a birthday present has come by sea mail and is waiting on the kitchen table. I run down the hill to see what it might be. There's a crumpled, mimeographed sheet of paper before me: APPROVAL OF LEAVE granted to Mr. R. L. Wendel, Education Officer II A, Songea Secondary School.

For weeks we've been hoping for this. We need to be stateside before the fall school term to give us time to find other teaching jobs or get into grad school. The approval of Bob's leave now gives us release, and a chance to see some of Europe on the way home.

Once the news is out, a gaggle of our fellow teachers serenades us with Christmas carols. We join in and march around singing to other colleagues, ending up at Gil's for glasses of Tusker beer as homework sits unmarked on our table.

***

In class the boys are confused by the difference between "Do you like tea?" and "Do you want some tea?" In Swahili the same verb is used for "want" and "like." In their eyes if you like something, you want it.

***

Some of us here at the school have been making plans for President Nyerere's visit. We discuss several types of receptions, but given the numbers and facilities, have decided on *pulao*, a rice and meat dish that could easily be served to a crowd. We've researched the details to a T, but it now looks like the visit has been postponed.

Today we learn the President's visit has been canceled. If we can't see Nyerere we'll visit Will and Kay at the Mlale settlement on Saturday. It's difficult for them to drive to Songea with their three children, so we'll go out for lunch and I'll bring the food. Joseph bought a nice piece of goat yesterday, so I'll make a French lamb stew with vegetables, a cucumber soup and rum babas.

Rum Babas

3 tablespoons warm milk

1 teaspoon active dry yeast

3 large eggs (6 fl. oz. or ¾ cup liquid eggs)

1 tablespoon sugar

½ teaspoon salt

8 oz. (1¾ cups) bread flour

2 oz. (½ stick) unsalted butter

1. Soften yeast in 3 tablespoons lukewarm milk in bottom of mixing bowl.

2. When yeast has dissolved, mix in beaten eggs, sugar and salt. Stir in flour and let rest 15 minutes.

3. Slice butter over top of dough and knead using a dough hook for 10 minutes, or knead by hand by slapping the dough against the side of the bowl and pulling it back. The dough should take on the consistency of a shiny, satiny elastic mass. It will be soft.

4. Cover with a plate or plastic wrap and allow to rise until doubled and light, 1 ½ to 2 hours.

5. Butter 12-16 muffin cups or baba molds. Deflate dough and divide by even spoonfuls into the buttered cups. Smooth the tops with damp fingertips. Cover with a tea towel and let rise for an hour or until light. Mist tops with water before baking. (note: after the first rising, the dough may be deflated, covered with plastic wrap and refrigerated overnight. If refrigerated the second rising before

baking will take 2 hours.)

6. Bake at 400° 15-18 minutes or until richly golden brown.

7. Remove from tins and cool on a rack.

Rum syrup

24 fl. oz. (3 cups) water
10½ oz. (1½ cups) sugar
2-4 tablespoons dark rum
1 teaspoon vanilla
Apricot glaze (optional)

1. Combine water and sugar. Stir and bring to a strong boil. Remove thin syrup from heat. Cool slightly before adding rum and vanilla.

2. Place cool babas in the warm syrup turning them on both sides so each cake is fully saturated. Prick babas with a toothpick to encourage absorption. Babas will swell and lighten as they are infused with syrup. Allow babas to drain on a rack placed over a baking sheet. (Strain any crumbs from syrup and use for poaching fruit or reduce and use to sweeten berries.)

3. For a shiny surface, brush the syrup infused cakes with melted, apricot jam.

4. Serve with whipped cream and berries or poached pineapple.

Things begin in a dither. Joseph is late and doesn't have vegetables ready for me to put in the stew when I return from morning classes. Worse, we burn the first batch of onions and have to peel a bunch of thimble-sized onions to start all over again. Bob gets into a snit about my preparing the entire meal from soup to nuts, but Kay hasn't time to boil a potato.

Once we're settled in Kay's dining room, she brings out a chilled bottle of French white wine. The cooked cucumber soup is as delicate as it's refreshing, followed by a small onion and anchovy tart, sort of a French pizza. Then comes our mutton (goat) stew with carrots, green beans and potatoes. Will and Kay join us in mopping up the gravy with French bread. Little rum cakes make a tidy dessert, and Kay serves us Tia Maria with coffee. It rains for two hours while we dine in a cloud of wine, cakes, and a phonograph recording of Irish folk songs.

As we slither along the road from Mlale, we slide to a stop and inch over a pole bridge that crosses a rain-swollen stream below a hill. The rain has turned the hill as slippery as a playground slide. We keep rolling back onto the rickety bridge and half the time we skid off the bridge's track onto bare poles. Scared sober, I step out of the car and try my best to push. I'm not much help but notice a Land Rover facing us atop the hill. I wave and yell till the car full of barefoot Africans scramble down to help. Eight of us struggling, mud-splattered, finally lift the rear wheels and shove old Zelda up the hill. We wave goodbye to the Rover-load.

The rest of the trip isn't quite "downhill," but it's smooth despite pond-sized puddles we plow through and bogs we swerve over. A perfect double rainbow emerges, and we drive under its spectral arch from Peramiho to Songea.

When we get out of the car to photograph the sky, we see a young African woman wrapped in *kangas* with a basket of corn flour on her head and a baby on her back walking down the road. She asks for a ride, we say *Ndiyo* (yes), and all four pile into the car.

* * *

Friday afternoon as I'm puttering in the kitchen, schoolboys on the football field behind our house break into song and dance. I listen till I can't stay inside any longer. I join them, stamping out rhythms and singing Swahili words the meaning of which I haven't a clue. The boys are chanting and shuffling with no accompaniment; the simplest drum would be out of place.

Bob is busy packing. I may have to live out of a shoebox for our last weeks. After Bob finds a pile of wood powder next to one of our *Wadendiuli* drums, we worry they might have termites. We hope to get home with more than dust.

***

Sometimes while I'm in class the rain barrels down leaving a shallow lake on the school compound and an irrigation ditch–sized creek trickling down the hill toward our house. It's senseless to walk home with shoes on, so I join the boys, slip off my sandals and splash home barefoot. The damp ground is warm after the rain; the grass is lettuce-soft and sometimes I wade in the ditch creek to feel tepid water over my toes.

***

About 4:30 Bob leaves to deliver some Mbeya food and to stop at Noel's to work on the car. I cook supper and sit down with Thackeray's *Vanity Fair.* The sudden rain lashes with such force I feel our house is going to tumble to rubble. After an hour of monsoonal downpour, by six it's too dark to read, and the lights don't come on. There's scarcely a second between rounds of thunder cracks. Lightning hits so close it seems to leap into the house, and the light bulbs ping. Our front yard becomes a lake, even though it's on a slope. This concrete foundation house could be washed away. I refuse to stand in front of the window. I pace up and down the hall and wonder if I should hide under the bed.

In the kitchen I light a solitary candle and keep looking out the window for Bob. I think of Will who stopped by to pick up his Mbeya food an hour ago and headed for Mlale in an old topless Land Rover. Twice I slam the door after the wind whips it open. I set about making pastry. As I roll out a pie shell there's a crash at the door. Bob's back.

The torrent continues all night. This morning Joseph tells me quite a few African homes were washed away, and one man was struck by lightning.

* * *

It's St. Patrick's Day. With Irishmen in residence in this corner of East Africa, I ready a stack of goodie boxes for the Paddys. I wrap some old chalk boxes in green paper, line them with doilies and fill them with fruitcake and green divinity.

* * *

A new letter on the school wall magazine claims many boys have failed English on the Cambridge exam because they study under Americans who do not know proper British English. This news brings me to a slow boil; I've become fairly expert in grammar and usage. There may be different word preferences such as "truck" or "lorry," "gas" or "petrol," but British and American grammar use the same standards. Nevertheless, the boys are adamant. Worst of all, we suspect the letter comes from an anti-American staff member. It's too well written to be a schoolboy's editorial.

* * *

Bob entrusts a new notebook to Yusof, suggesting the schoolboys might leave us a few farewell comments. He drops by this afternoon to tell us the notebook has been stolen. We're baffled.

I all but weep out loud while Yusof explains about the book of farewells. He gazes at us warmly and says, "Yes, perhaps this is the same way Christ felt when he tried so hard to do good and the people just condemned him. We Africans are truly a long way from civilization."

Bob and I have a talk with our headmaster, Paul. When we tell him we want to leave here with good memories, he nods. I say we should get together for dinner on Thursday evening.

* * *

In class this morning it's hard to look some students in the eye. Later, a letter arrives from one of last year's schoolboys now studying in Iringa at the Lutheran High School. He writes, "Sir, I may be truer if I say you were more to me as a personal friend than a mere teacher or house master. Sir, I thank you very much for your assistance you gave me. Remember me to your wife, Mary Jo. Tell her that I say without her I could not have tasted pineapple cake which only few people can prepare."

* * *

Tomorrow I'll have a typhoid shot. I deserve at least one sick day this term, and the injection may be my excuse.

Compositions are hard to grade, and students raise an outcry that I'm unfair. They claim too many people always get the same mark; they say the same students get high marks. I must stop putting comments on their papers. I'm not going to argue with them. I've had way too much guff from the boys lately.

* * *

As we trudge home after Saturday morning classes Yusof runs up to us waving a new green notebook. He says one of the boys has offered this as a replacement for the stolen book of farewells.

"Whose book is this?" Bob asks.

"Sir, it's from Zoro," he says meaning Bernard known to his friends as Zoro, the slowest boy in the slowest class.

A notebook may not sound like much, but it's a treasure here where paper is scarce and a notebook costs more than three pounds of meat. We stare at the notebook. We don't know what to say. Later when we speak with Bernard, trying to express our gratitude, we say we feel we should not take his book. We see his face fall.

Bernard, with gap teeth and hunched shoulders, is the same student who approached me on the school grounds months ago asking for names of some of my American women friends. He claimed he wanted to have an American woman as a pen pal, saying he would like to marry someone like me. When I replied that my friends would be much too old for him, he looked at the ground. "Oh, madam, you do not know how old I am."

It's true, some of our students could be older than Bob or myself.

* * *

We chat with our headmaster, Paul, when he comes for dinner. He sees the drums next to the fireplace in our sitting room, chuckles and says, "You know, my people would really laugh at me if I put one of these things in my house." Drums are everyday necessities; to show off a drinking basket or a water gourd as decorations in an African sitting room would be as strange as Americans lining pots and pans on the mantle. It dawns on me why Joseph decorated his front room with a strainer, hot water bottle and shoes. If an African family has a refrigerator, Paul says, it will be smack in the middle of the sitting room in full view.

Paul goes on to tell us that many of our students have girlfriends. The Christians must do their courting in secret at home during the holidays. The Moslems often live with women during their vacations. When they return to school they're not allowed to have any contact with girls.

APRIL 1965

Sleepless for hours, I get up and take aspirin. It doesn't help. About three a.m. someone raps on our door, calling, "Mr. Wendel! Mr. Wendel!"

Bob's asleep. The voice calls out again, this time with a hard edge, an African voice growing more strident with every "Mr. Wendel!" I don't know any villagers who would use Bob's last name.

Could it be one of the African teachers? I walk near the door, "Zakao?" I ask. But whoever it is continues knocking, calling, "Mr. Wendel! Mr. Wendel!"

I rouse Bob, who lifts the curtain. He says he can't see anyone. He grabs the flashlight and stumbles out our front door, all but knocking into Jonah, the school carpenter. "Oh, Mr. Wendel, my wife is about to get a baby just now. Could you please take us to hospital?"

Bob pulls on trousers and a sweater over his pajamas, slips on some shoes, and heads out. I lie back in bed, but before long I hear Zelda's sputtering return. Apparently, Bob has had trouble understanding Jonah's wild Swahili but has concluded that the idea of going to the hospital was Jonah's; his wife was unwilling to set foot in a place with doctors and nurses. We assume Mrs. Jonah upped and left for the local midwife. When Jonah questioned a neighbor about his wife's whereabouts, he was told that she was *tayari sasa hivi* (ready just now) and afraid to get into a car.

212

***

We sell our hens. At first we don't think we'll be able to get anything for them, and Bob isn't about to eat his pets. Joe says he'll give us ten shillings; Mike offers twenty. Joe's houseboy, Alius, scoots over and hands us the grand total of thirty shillings. He wants them for breeding. He'll get a year's worth of eggs for the price of chicken feed.

***

When I wake this morning, it looks as though it's snowing, with a cloud cover of drizzle drifting down the slope toward our house, enveloping the school.

***

After dinner Friday night Bob and I pop over to Maisie's. She's asked me to come by some evening and show her how to make chocolate fudge. I've had great results with this recipe, and everyone wants to learn it. The trick of adding cream of tartar assures creamy fudge.

Fudge

14 oz. (2 cups) sugar
1½ oz. (6 tablespoons) unsweetened cocoa
⅛ teaspoon each salt and cream of tartar
8 fl. oz. (1 cup) milk
1 oz. (2 tablespoons) butter
1 teaspoon vanilla

1. In a heavy saucepan whisk sugar, cocoa, salt, cream of tartar until lumps are removed. Butter a large loaf pan or line the pan with plastic wrap.

2. Blend milk into sugar and cocoa mixture; stir over moderate heat until the sugar is dissolved. Remove sugar crystals on the pan sides using a pastry brush dipped in water. Cook slowly to a soft ball (235° F or test by dropping hot syrup into iced water). Do not stir during this slow boil which may take 15-20 minutes. (note: check thermometer accuracy in water which boils at 212° F)

3. Remove fudge from heat; add butter. Cool until warm (place hand comfortably on bottom of saucepan); add vanilla. Using a wooden spoon, stir until fudge begins to thicken. Scoop and smooth into the prepared pan to firm up. If fudge "sugars" or is too soft, heat 2 oz. milk in a saucepan, add the fudge and recook to the soft ball. Often twice cooked fudge is the best ever.

***

Even after the stiff gin and tonic Maisie gave me, I have trouble getting to sleep. Today is my last day of classes. I decide to read to my students. All week I've thought about Guy de Maupassant's tale, "The Piece of String," which I found in the school library. The story is about how an honest man is ruined by others' lies and suspicions. This certainly sounds familiar after the shenanigans at the school lately. Bob warns me my students won't grasp de Maupassant's narrative, but of course I don't listen. I recite the story in twenty minutes and simplify the difficult words.

The students sit still and appear to be captivated, but during a discussion afterwards, I realize the story's theme goes over their heads. I end up doing a lot of explaining, then try to read aloud James Weldon Johnson's "The Creation," which they think is a big joke and laugh so hard I don't finish it.

When I meet my French class for the last time, I bring in some crusty baguettes as a treat. Later, of course my other students accuse "Mrs. Wendel" of being "unfair, favoring her French class." By now I'm so sick of their pettiness that I don't give a damn. The students who have volunteered to take French have worked a lot harder than the others; they deserve a reward, be it ever so simple as a dry chunk of bread. When it's almost time for the bell, we sing and dance to "*Alouette.*"

* * *

Saturday afternoon we drive out the Lindi Road to visit two American Peace Corpsmen camped in a tent. They're doing spadework, surveying a road through the bush. They tell us they'll be busy in the area till September of next year. They're diligent all right, though they hear most of their Peace Corps pals elsewhere in Tanzania are spending more time at the beach than they are on the Lindi Road.

We're ready leave them when a little *toto* (child) unexplainably runs up with the *zawadi* (gift) of a giant cucumber. It's eleven inches long, fourteen inches around and weighs as much as a small Hubbard squash. It's almost impossible to get slicing cucumbers here since Tanzanians feel the bigger they are the better they taste.

* * *

People are getting deported right and left. A *Time* correspondent was kicked out of Uganda last week. Today we hear that two American consulate workers have been sent back to the U.S.A. for "subversive" activity. Nyerere has come out in support of the Congo Coalition leader Tshombe, and Tanzania has begun having diplomatic relations with Communist North Korea.

* * *

The saga of our farewell notebook hits a new low. Bernard comes up to me after an exam and asks to bring the book down to us since it's nearly finished. We don't set a time, and he probably stops by while we're at the Peace Corps camp. When Bob returns from bed check that night, he says, "I guess somebody hates us." Apparently, Bernard's locked box with our book of farewells has been broken into, and the second book has been stolen. I take a sleeping pill and wonder if our house will be pillaged.

More than any other souvenir Bob and I hoped to bring home Bernard's book of farewells. I stop one of my 3A students who will give me a candid view of the situation. I'm relieved to learn that the theft occurred not because anyone disliked us, but more because of jealousies among the students who wanted the notebook themselves.

To top things off: some students think we're paying Bernard for the autographed notebook. His friend says this must be why the book was stolen from Yusof earlier. The boys thought Bob was planning to give Yusof a special gift for overseeing the book.

Later Bob confers with Paul. Our disappointment doesn't matter; Paul will resolve things.

* * *

After my final English exam this morning, I have stacks of papers to grade.

In the afternoon Bob and I stroll over for a chat with our new Indian teacher. Mr. Agawald, a sixtyish widower, has taught from Bombay to Mombasa for the past thirty years. He has a grown family and grandchildren in India. We invite him for supper. He's a Hindu vegetarian, so I'll have a chance to put my Gujarati cookery to use. The other day I made him some potato *bhajias* (fritters); he said they were delectable.

* * *

If anyone wants permanent hair dye, I can recommend ballpoint pen ink. I wonder if I'll ever get the red blobs out of my hair from the broken pen I accidentally brushed by my head. I've given myself two shampoos, a steam oil treatment and tried toothbrush-scrubbing my stained locks with Tide and laundry bleach. Nothing works.

***

We'll have the Zulu House end-of-term party tonight, then a school *baraza* tomorrow morning when we'll see the students for the last time. Two schoolboys are in our kitchen now slicing fourteen loaves of bread to make jam sandwiches. I planned to bake two sheet cakes, but I'm low on shortening and out of powdered sugar. So I've turned sweet roll dough into an assortment of buns. I've finished our supply of cinnamon and sprinkled in other spices plus grated orange rind. I'd better help clean up. The boys are through licking the margarine tins and eating the end crusts of bread.

I hate long goodbyes. We'll be expected to give speeches, brief farewells letting bygones be bygones. One thing I'd like to say: I hope I've given them an example of women in the Western world. Most of my students think women are capable of little more than pounding cassava and bearing children. Perhaps they will think of me and discover new ways of seeing their mothers, sisters and the women they will marry.

Tonight Bob and I hike down to the river below our house. The locals have planted rice that looks like tall grass topped with heads of loose grain. We notice a dozen or so reed lean-tos on the side of the hill, where groups of women and kids have set up housekeeping by their fields for the season.

As their rice grows, they must shoo birds out of the fields or there will be nothing left to harvest. They've devised a clever scheme.

They've planted large branches as fake trees in straight lines across their rice fields. They tie the fake trees together with bark strips. Someone stands at one end of the field pulling on the bark, and all the trees sway back and forth in unison, scaring away the scavengers.

* * *

At our Friday night tea party one of the schoolboys, thanking me for goodies I've made, announces, "The smell of these foods will not go out of our heads until we die." Bob gives a rousing speech, and we shake hands with the boys—Abdulla, Isaack, Mwidadi, Simon, Juma—as they leave. Saturday morning, and throughout the day after the final *baraza,* gangs of students knock on our door. Bernard, who tried to give us the second Book of Farewells, breaks into tears telling us he feels awful about what happened. We chat with him, hoping to heal his hurt. He wonders if we might have time to visit his home near Peramiho before we leave. We've planned one last trip to the mission anyway and agree to meet him near the mission hospital office.

* * *

After we pick up our mended shoes from the cobbler, we drive Bernard to Lipinyapinya, a cluster of mud huts hidden by brush and trees.

We pull off the road and make our way down a path through a cornfield to the family compound. We meet Bernard's father, wrinkled as a raisin, seated on a wooden chair in front of his hut. Bernard claims his dad is seventy-nine. The old man tells us he has seventeen children with two wives. White hair fringes his jawbone, and he has on a white skullcap and a long green gown. Bernard leads us to a well-swept mud brick dwelling. We step over the threshold and stoop through three doorways until we enter an airy room with a small table and four wooden chairs set out for us. Bernard has been using his brother's house during school holidays. The walls display posters I've noticed at the school, as well as the usual shoes, scraps of Christmas wrapping paper, an Aga film sign and the family collection of photos.

After leading his father by the hand, Bernard carries in a large tray with a cracked teapot and four yellow cups. He serves us white rolls and milky tea. We have trouble convincing the old man to drink tea with us. It's not the African custom to eat with visitors when they come to a village, even as we remember our first foray into a village for Saidi's wedding and we were served our meal separately from the villagers. Because the bread is hard and the tea sweet, I suggest dunking the dry rolls into the tea. They're surprised, almost shocked at this notion, but soon gesture and smile, letting us know that dunking is a good idea.

Just as we set down our teacups, Bernard's mother and his older sister join us. We pull a few gifts out of a basket: an empty five-pound milk tin with the fitting lid, packages of Dentine, balloons and a loaf of freshly baked bread. Most people here relish ordinary bread; one person alone will finish a whole loaf without butter or jam.

I see the old man's eyes bug when I blow up a purple balloon. He bats it with his fists, chattering like a little kid.

* * *

Bob has organized the packing, and I've filled tins with cookies and snacks for our journey to Dar. The fridge is gone. Marie can use my leftover waxed paper and aluminum foil. Joseph's been taking home baskets of towels, bedding and curtains. Marie and Maisie have given us dinner the past two nights.

* * *

Friday evening we take a long last stroll around the school. Lacy jacaranda branches sway over the parade ground, the school generator ticks on and the bittersweet smell of wood smoke from cooking fires fills the air. There have been days when Songea loomed like a world without end. Now like the shrill blast of a twisting schoolboy's police whistle that has fallen silent, our dance is over.

At 7:30 on the Saturday morning before Easter, we nudge Zelda down the school drive and face the Njombe Road.

Clockwise from top: Zelda the car, Bob Wendel with
Joseph the houseboy, Bob and Mary Jo's residence in Songea.

Left to Right: Songea Secondary School classroom building,
Mary Jo and two students.

ABOUT THE AUTHOR

A native of rural western Colorado, Mary Jo McMillin learned to bake as soon as she learned to read. As a teenager, she cooked for family, friends, school and church groups.

She attended Colorado State College where she worked in the dining hall, gained two degrees and fell under the spell of French cooking when she helped with a professor's dinner parties. At twenty-one, she married her college beau, Robert Wendel, and the following year they signed on with Teachers for East Africa. Living in both East and West Africa expanded her world view, and put her in touch with culinary customs beyond Western culture.

When her two children were young, McMillin catered small events and taught cooking classes. She wrote regular food features for the Dekalb *Daily Chronicle* and the Hamilton *Journal-News.*

In 1986 she launched Mary Jo's Cuisine. The small, magic cottage soon became the dining destination of Oxford, Ohio. Heralded by major publications, reviewers, and culinary professionals, the restaurant was known for exquisite taste and exceptional quality. Following the close of the business in 2004, McMillin published *Mary Jo's Cuisine: A Cookbook* (Orange Frazer Press, 2007).

Since moving to the North Shore in 2008 with her second husband, poet James Reiss, to be near her children and grandchildren, McMillin continues to keep active as a chef. She teaches small group cooking classes, caters for private clients and blogs at *Mary Jo's Kitchen* https://mjcuisine.wordpress.com. She also maintains a long-standing professional relationship with the Ballymaloe Cookery School in Ireland with teaching sojourns.

RECIPE INDEX

*Recipes have been updated

BIBLIOGRAPHY

Darley, James M.. *Map of Tanganyika: Atlas Plate 54.* 1960.
The National Geographic Society, Washington, D.C..
National Geographic Magazine, 118.3 September 1960: n. pag. Print.

CPSIA information can be obtained
at www.ICGtesting.com
Printed in the USA
FFOW03n1408170118
44581369-44466FF